MALDIVES
PEOPLE AND ENVIRONMENT

By Paul A. Webb

Photography by Elke Seeger and Paul A Webb.
Additional photographs and text by Dr. Chas Anderson and Dr. Dennis Adams.

Published by

 Media Transasia Limited

14th Floor, Orakarn Building
26 Chidlom Road, Ploenchit Bangkok 10500, Thailand

Text: Paul A. Webb
Photographs: Elke Seeger and Paul A. Webb
Additional photographs and text: Dr. Chas Anderson and
Dr. Dennis Adams.

ﺑﺴﻢ ﺍﻟﻠﻪ ﺍﻟﺮﺣﻤﻦ ﺍﻟﺮﺣﻴﻢ

މުގައްދިމާ

ވެރި،

ދިވެހިރާއްޖެ

ރައީސުލް

ދިވެހިރާއްޖޭގެ މަހުކަމާ މިސްތަކަރ ފިޔަ ވެ ތައްޔާރުކުރެއްވިގެ މިވެލިފޮޅިޔަ، ރާއްޖޭ އާއި ރާއްޖޭގެ މިހުނާންގެ އާދަޔާ ތަރައްޤީ މަހުކަމަ އޭނާ ހިތަހިކަމަ އުފެދުރުއިގެ ވެވޮތީ ޝައުޤުވެރި ކަމާއި ކައުނީ ސަބަބުތަކާ، ފުން މިހުންމުމުން މައިރާމާ ހިސާބުތުވެ ބޮތަން، އާއި ރާއްޖޭގެ އެ ވުއެ ބަހައަތާ ފަރާތު ތަރައްވޮއެވެ. އަދި އޭނާ ކަންކަންމުވަމަ އޭ ވެދު މިސްތަކަމޔ ދިވިއެއްފޮއި ހުހާ ފާޢުވެލާއި މަހުކަން މިސްނުރޮއި، ދިސެޓާ ހަތައްޒު ވައުވެއެއެ. ފޮތިގެ މުބަސްނަފޮއި މިވަސަސެހާ ފުޅުކައުވޮން އާމް ހުރަ އެ ރައ އަޅުކަސުއަ ސަތުރުޅޮން ފޮޅިރަ މުޅޮ ކަހަޔ އެޅޮވެ. އަދި ޔާކޮޅަ ކާ ޢުޅަ އެނޮރެކުސަށާ ރާއްޖޭގޮޅާހަ އަޅިޔާ ބިހައޅޮއި މިސްތަކާ ޝޮމޭލފޮއިގެ ބޮޅާން، ރާއްޖޭގެ ކާސެވާއިޢޮ މަހުކަން، ކާމޮޅެން ފިއަރެ އޔޮރެސޮ އެޅާފާ ޝޮކޮޅާ ފޮޅޮ ފޮޅޮޅާ ރޮހޮޅޮ ޅޮ ފޮޮޅޮ ރ، ދިސެޓާ ފޮހޮ ޅޮ ޮޅޮ ޮޮ ޅޮ ޮޮ ޮޮ ޅޮ ޮޮ ޮޮ، ފޮހޮ ޮޮ ޮޅޮ ޮޮ ޮޅޮ ޮޮ ޮޮ ޮޅ.

"ދިވެހިރާއްޖެ - ދިވެހިންނާ ދިވެހި ވިޖޯހާ" މިފޮޅޮޅޮ ޮޮޅޮ ޅޮ ޮޅޮ މަހުކަން ޮޮ ޮޮ ޮޮޅޮ ޅޮ ޮޅޮ ޮޮ ޮޮ ޮޮ ޮޮ ޮޮ ޮޮ ޮޮ ޮޮ ޮޮ ޮޮ ޮޮ ޮޮ، ޮޅޮ ޮޅޮ ޮޮ ޮޅޮ ޮޮ ޮޮ ޮޮ ޮޮ ޮޮ، ޮޮ ޮޅޮ ޮޮ ޮޅޮ ޮޮ ޮޮ ޮޮ، ޮޮ ޮޮ ޮޮ ޮޅޮ ޮޮ ޮޮ ޮޮ ޮޮ، ރާއްޖޭގެ މަހުކަން ޮޮ ޮޮ ޮޅޮ ޮޮ ޮޮ ޮޮ ޮޮ ދިސެޓާ ޮޮ ޮޅޮ، ޮޮ ޮޮޅޮ ޮޮ ޮޮ ޮޮ ޮޮ ޅޮ ޮޮ ޮޮ.

22 ރަބީޢުލްއައްވަލު 1409

2 ނޮވެމްބަރ 1988

މައުމޫން ޢަބްދުލްޤައްޔޫމް

ދިވެހިރާއްޖޭގެ ރައީސުލްޖުމްހޫރިއްޔާ

MULEE-AAGE

Malé, Republic of Maldives

2 November 1988

INTRODUCTION

This beautiful book on the Maldives by Mr. Paul Webb is the result of the author's keen personal interest in the country, its people and its traditions. In the course of collecting material for this book, Mr. Webb travelled to many islands of the Republic and carefully studied the small island-communities and their way of life. I am happy that my government was able to extend all possible assistance to the author in his work. A chapter on marine life of the Maldives by Dr. Charles Anderson and another on our plant life by Dr. Dennis Adams add variety and depth to Mr. Webb's valuable work.

I am sure Maldives: its People and Environment will provide very useful information to anyone interested in learning more about this nation of islands. My thanks go to Mr. Webb and his associates for the commendable attempt they have made to depict my count'ry and its people in a manner that does justice to a unique and rich culture.

Maumoon Abdul Gayoom
President of the Republic of Maldives

Acknowledgement

Without the personal support and encouragement of His Excellency, Maumoon Abdul Gayoom, the President of the Republic of Maldives, the production of this book would have been impossible. The President's sympathy for the environment is reflected in the pages of this book.

Mr. Abdul Rasheed Hussain — Executive Secretary to the President — has been a major influence in bringing the project to a successful end. His advice, encouragement and hard work have been invaluable over the years.

The Ministry of Atolls Administration had the unfortunate task of looking after the author over a period of three years and supplying his somewhat erratic demands. The Minister, Mr. Hameed, and his Senior Undersecretary, also Mr. Hameed, made the impossible very possible and supplied the facilities and goodwill to make the project realistic. Many other Maldivians have helped over the years: Mrs. Ameena Hameed of the President's Office has been a constant friend and supporter. Ali Shafeeg of the Ministry of Agriculture, Abdulla Shougee of Atolls Administration, both worked hard on the project.

From a production point of view, Dr. Dennis Adams and Dr. Chas Anderson have both made a significant contribution.

Finally the author would like to thank the people of the Maldives for showing that there is still a simple world where crime and violence are unknown and there is always a smile for a stranger.

Paul A. Webb

MALDIVES
PEOPLE AND ENVIRONMENT

INTRODUCTION

The Maldives. To many, even the name is unfamiliar, and to most completely unknown. This tiny country has managed to slip by the mainstream of world politics and history, and been largely unaffected by world events that have shaped and formulated the rest of our world.

Such events as the conquest of the globe by the Mongol hordes of Genghis Khan, the invention of the automobile, two world wars and the splitting of the atom have left the Maldives virtually unaffected, except perhaps as a lesson in history.

However 15 years ago the curtain that had hid the Maldives for so many centuries was finally pulled back forever, when Europeans and others discovered these islands as a superb tourist destination to get away from the vagaries of the European winter, and as the curtain has come open it has revealed a country with unique traditions and a history stretching back to a time hidden in the mists of antiquity.

A land of Sultans and Sultanas with a lineage traceable back to the time of Buddha; a dynastic family the rival of many other cultures in the world, with a history of such powerful interest and moment that it could have been written as a novel. A history of invasion, intrigue and perhaps one of the first guerilla organisations in the world, fighting a bloody battle of liberation to throw off the chains of foreign oppression in a struggle that finally resulted in a lasting freedom. A religious history that has seen Islam triumph over Buddhism and stood the test of a foreign power determined to convert the people to Christianity at the point of a gun. A colourful and sometimes tragic story of the birth pangs of a small unknown country in

9

the midst of the Indian Ocean.

The very geography of the Maldives is unique, somewhere between 1,100 and 2,000 small islands spread over a great expanse of the Indian Ocean and each inhabited island with a separate personality and a way of life that has not changed in hundreds of years.

The populations inhabiting the remote islands are perhaps some of the only people left in the world today who are surviving totally on their immediate environment. The very last remnants of a way of life and a society that disappeared from most cultures 300 years ago.

With tourism has come an inevitable change, a rush forward into the 20th century for many Maldivians, but still in the remoter island things are much as they ever were and this book records an environment and a way of life that will no doubt change with the benefits and disadvantages of tourism. It also records an environment that up till now remains absolutely pristine with not a vestige of industrial or other pollution to mar what must be truly the last 'lost paradise'.

Left and above: Life on the remote islands.

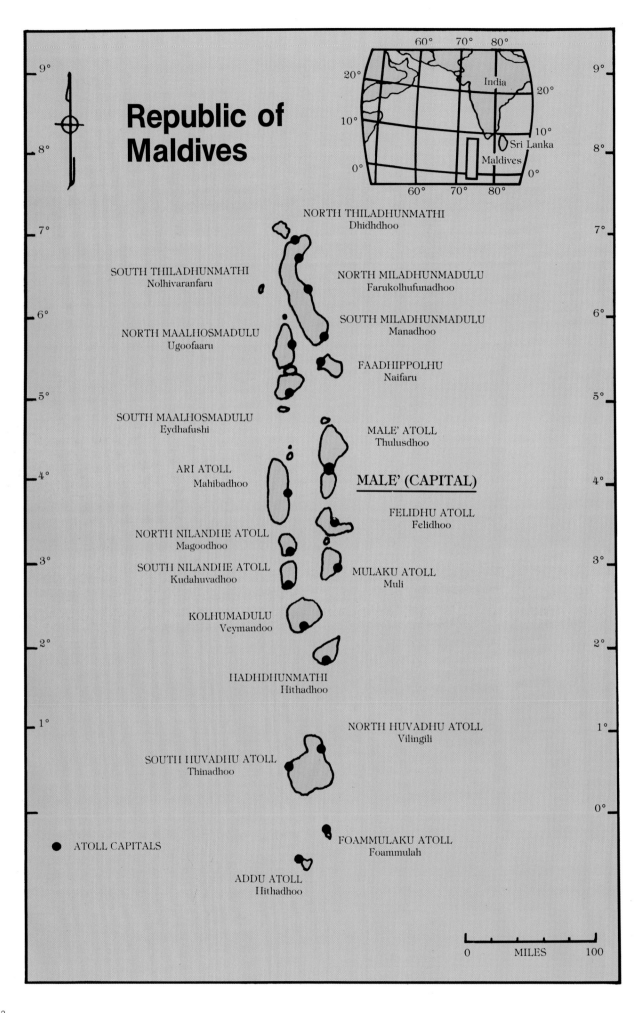

Republic of Maldives

60° 70° 80°

20° India 20°

10° 10°

Sri Lanka

0° Maldives 0°

60° 70° 80°

NORTH THILADHUNMATHI
Dhidhdhoo

SOUTH THILADHUNMATHI
Nolhivaranfaru

NORTH MILADHUNMADULU
Farukolhufunadhoo

SOUTH MILADHUNMADULU
Manadhoo

NORTH MAALHOSMADULU
Ugoofaaru

FAADHIPPOLHU
Naifaru

SOUTH MAALHOSMADULU
Eydhafushi

MALE' ATOLL
Thulusdhoo

ARI ATOLL
Mahibadhoo

MALE' (CAPITAL)

FELIDHU ATOLL
Felidhoo

NORTH NILANDHE ATOLL
Magoodhoo

SOUTH NILANDHE ATOLL
Kudahuvadhoo

MULAKU ATOLL
Muli

KOLHUMADULU
Veymandoo

HADHDHUNMATHI
Hithadhoo

NORTH HUVADHU ATOLL
Vilingili

SOUTH HUVADHU ATOLL
Thinadhoo

● ATOLL CAPITALS

FOAMMULAKU ATOLL
Foammulah

ADDU ATOLL
Hithadhoo

0 MILES 100

THE LAND. GEOGRAPHY AND GEOLOGY

A careful look at a good map will reveal a chain of islands located partly north, and partly south of the Equator, between 7 6′ 30″ and 0 41′ 48″ south and between 72 32′ 30″ and 73 45′ 54″ east of Greenwich, that seem to rise up out of the ocean in defiance of the hostile environment that surrounds them.

The markings on the map are not actual islands, they are Atolls (Atoll = atolu, a word derived from Dhivehi, the Maldivian language) and only on old British Admiralty charts is the incredible amount of islands visible — somewhere between 1,100 and 2,000. Confusion has always existed concerning the number of islands. Subject as they are to the elements of wind and wave power, some islands actually disappear whilst others are newly created. If the sandbars and coral outcrops are counted then the total is in excess of 2,000 but if the number is calculated only on islands with a vegetation cover then it is closer to 1,190.

Based on a vast submarine mountain range which extends southwards from the land mass of India, which also gives rise to the Laccadives and Minicoy in the north and the Chagos in the South (including the U.S. Airforce base of Diego Garcia). The Maldives owe their origin to the collapse of this mountain range over a great period of time.

It is still an argument in academic circles as to the origins of this type of coral oceanic island, but most authorities still put their weight behind the 150 year old theories of Charles Darwin, the father of the theory of

evolution. Darwin never visited the Maldives, but based much of his theory on the atoll formation of the country of which he had heard. As the range of mountains collapsed, individual higher peaks attracted and promoted the growth of corals, which thrive only in the warm and shallow oceans, and the growth of these corals into an encircling protective reef matched the gradual collapse of the mountain peak to which they clung with a tenacious grip. With the final collapse, a central lagoon was formed with its encircling reefs, and the coral growth on the seaward side of this structure was enhanced by fresh seawater, whilst coral growth on the lee side was somewhat restricted. It is thought that the bases of the present day reefs correspond to fringing reefs that were formed around these mountains when they were islands millions of years ago.

The main bone of contention concerning the formation of these coral structures is whether the sea rose and covered the mountains or whether the mountains sank under the sea. But for our purpose it is incidental as there are as many experts claiming the one theory to be right as there are the other.

The word to describe these coral island formations is atoll, and an atoll can be roughly classified as an almost circular reef that, in itself, encompasses a central lagoon with a top reef that is mostly exposed, forming small islands of accumulated coral sand and other debris. The Maldives boasts the largest true atoll formation in the world in the form of the Huvadhu atoll, in the south, which has a lagoon with an area of 2,240 km² and a diameter of 70 miles with a depth of 86 metres.

These atolls are reef forms of the open

Left, top: The 'dhonis' are hand built from local materials by master craftsmen and are sea worthy craft.

Bottom, left: The islands are remote communities and any arrival brings the whole village out to see who has come.

Bottom, right: Fishermen cleaning their catch before selling it at market. Fish is as important to the islanders as the coconut tree.

Right: Shy Maldivian girl peers out of the doorway under the protective arm of her mother.

sea. The outside reef can drop down hundreds, even thousands of feet, quite unlike platform reefs. They normally have one entrance across the reef, caused by tidal and wave action, and this is generally on the lee side.

Particular to the Maldives is the peculiar reef structure known as a 'faro' (another Dhivehi word. Both are in the English dictionary) consisting of a series of small circular reefs in a line, rather than the more lengthened reef crown of other atolls in the world.

The land structure of the islands of the Maldives is not often more than a metre above sea level, and if not for the protection of the outer ring reef the islands would soon wash away under the influence of the powerful swells of the Indian Ocean.

The Maldives are made up of 26 of these atoll formations, stretching from north to south for over 764 kilometres and at its widest point 128 kilometres across. The nearest landfall in any direction is to the north, India at 595 kilometres; to the north west at 670 kilometres is Sri Lanka and the Chagos group of islands due south at about 550 kilometres. For political convenience and local administration purposes the atolls of the Maldives are divided into 19 units.

THE ATOLLS OF THE MALDIVES
1. Thiladhunmathi Uthuruburi.
2. Thiladhunmathi Dhekunuburi.
3. Miladhunmadulu Uthuruburi.
4. Miladhunmadulu Dhekunuburi.
5. Maalhosmadulu Uthuruburi.
6. Maalhosmadulu Dhekunuburi.
7. Faadhipolhu atoll.
8. Malé atoll.
9. Ari atoll.
10. Felidhe atoll.
11. Mulaku atoll.
12. Nilandhe Uthuruburi.
13. Nilandhe Dhekunuburi.
14. Kolhumadulu.
15. Hadhunmathi.
16. Huvadu Uthuruburi.
17. Huvadu Dhekunuburi.
18. Foamulah.
19. Addu.

The geographical situation of the Maldives occupies an area of some 90,000 km².

The climate of a region plays a major role in its natural formation and these islands are no different, representing as they do tiny specks of life in a vast ocean area, making

them particularly susceptible to the elemental forces of nature. A sub-tropical climate with a temperature of between 25.5 — 30.4 C and almost always a gentle breeze blowing off the ocean from somewhere, the weather is both ideal and soporific for tourists and Maldivians alike, but because of their geographical position the islands are influenced by the Asian monsoon systems.

From May till about November or December the south-west monsoon sets in bringing the welcome heavy rains, which may flood the few roads but also fill the water tanks, and increase the cloud cover to an average of 60-70%. During this period strong winds and thunderstorms arrive from all directions and very often the sea is far too rough for safe voyaging. This south-west monsoon tends never to reach as far down as the southernmost atolls and some years, Addu atoll, at the tip of the Maldives escapes this monsoon.

In the far north it is a very different matter, as cyclonic storms and hurricanes have occasionally swept in at this time to

Left: 'Dhoni' crossing the shallow reef of an island.

Above, left: Tuna of this size are a common catch in Maldivian waters.

Right: Boat builders at work.

17

Top, left: Monsoon storms sweep across the atolls sometimes bringing welcome rain.

This page, left: The coconut palm is used by the islander extensively. Life without it would be unthinkable.

Top, right: Crystal clear turquoise lagoons of the Maldives, untouched by industrial pollution.

Bottom, left: A fishing 'dhoni' sets sail from an island.

devastate islands, particularly in Thiladhunmathi Uthuruburi and Thiladhunmathi Dhekunuburi atolls, but not so frequently in this century as in the last.

Ocean currents during the south-west monsoon run west to east at an average of 24 metres/minute, and reverse themselves during the north-east monsoon when they run at an average of 25-30 metres/minute.

The north-east monsoon arrives in January, after having travelled down from the Laccadives where it becomes set about November, and is usually preceeded by a fortnight of strong winds blowing from north to east with heavy rain squalls. Once the monsoon has arrived the central and northern atolls enjoy dry and mild weather with very little cloud cover (cloudiness 10-30%) and the sea is usually calm. However the south then receives most of its rainfall and seas can be rough and dangerous. By April the monsoon dies away and the whole region experiences a hot dry period until the arrival of the south-west monsoon.

Rainfall averages 2100 mm per year, but is notoriously fickle and recent years have seen prolonged periods of tropical downpour followed by total absence of rainfall for long periods.

Obviously the monsoons play a large part in the erosion and formation of islands and this is partly why there is so much confusion about the number of islands actually existing. For instance, after a severe monsoon storm, three new islands were formed in the lagoon of Farukolhufunadhoo (Miladhunmadulu Uthuruburi atoll) in 1955, and the list of islands that have been washed away, by winds and waves, is almost endless. The island of Kilisfaruhuraa (Miladhunmadulu Uthuruburi atoll) was abandoned in 1973

because erosion had become so bad that the island seemed destined to sink beneath the waves.

It is obvious, if one compares the discrepancies between the figures of geographical area and actual land area, that much of the Maldives is sea. Because of the atoll formations, forming as they do a protective ring against the ocean around the large central lagoon, the sea in the interior is almost always calm and shallow. Outside these protective atolls there is nothing but open ocean and travel between these 19 atolls can at times be uncomfortable and sometimes extremely dangerous.

Many channels are narrow, but channels such as the Equatorial and the One and a Half Degree channel (so called because of its position on the map) are both very wide and deep. The Equatorial channel, known locally as the Addu Kandu, between Seenu and Huvadu atolls is about 74 kilometres wide and has a depth of more than a 1000 fathoms and currents of almost six knots. The One

and a Half Degree channel is 96 kilometres across and can only be crossed in a large seaworthy craft. In 1921 three small boats from the southernmost atoll of Addu, making their way to trade in Malé (the capital), were swept away by currents in the One and a Half Degree channel, and carried westwards across the Indian Ocean until they reached the coast of East Africa. Their families had given them up as lost forever when they suddenly turned up, back in the Maldives in 1922, after being shipped by a cargo vessel via Sri Lanka and this is by no means an isolated example.

The Maldivians, quite rightly, consider themselves as master seamen and when one considers that one of their small handbuilt wooden boats is capable of crossing many thousands of kilometres of open ocean without mishap then it is a true tribute to their seamanship and their sturdy little craft.

Left, top: The Indian Ocean breaking on the atoll reefs behind a fishing 'dhoni'.

This page, top: With primitive tools and only using hand and eye this man will produce a boat capable of crossing the Indian Ocean.

Left, bottom: Woman preparing husk to be used for rope making.

This page, right: Heavy storms can flood the capitals' roads quickly.

CALENDER OF MALDIVES HISTORY

1153.
> The country adopts Islam after the visit of a respected Muslim saint. The first Sultan was Muhammad ul-Adil

1343 & 1346.
> The famous Arab traveller, Abu Abdallah Muhammad (better known as Ibn. Batuta, the Moor of Tangier) visited the islands and stayed for some time. His writings on the country are well known.

1513.
> First violent contact with the Portugese who attacked Malé and subsequently built a fort with the consent of the Sultan, Kalu Muhammad, (1518). The Portugese were eventually thrown out with the aid of the Ali Raja of Cochin.

1558.
> Malé captured by the Portugese under the command of Adiri Adirin and held until 1573 when the Portugese were all killed by the Maldivian hero, Muhammad Takurufanu.

1602.
> The French adventurer and traveller, Pyrard de Laval, shipwrecked on the islands when his ship, the 'Corbin' ran aground. He stayed for seven years and his account of the Maldives at that time caused a sensation in Europe.

1609.
> Malé once again was attacked this time by pirates who killed Sultan, Ibrahim III, and caused considerable damage to the capital.

1631.
> Attempt by the Portugese to storm Malé, which ended in failure when they were driven off with great losses.

1649.
> Final futile assault on Malé by the Portugese who were driven off by heavy cannon fire from the fort.

1752.

The Ali Raja of Malabar attacked Malé with a fleet of ships. After setting fire to many of the buildings and ransacking the palace, the pirates stayed for a few months until the Maldivians under the leadership of Hassan Manikufanu threw them out. The Ali Raja continued to lay siege to Malé until eventually driven away with the help of a fleet of French Men O'War under the command of Monsieur le Termellier. He was known with affection by the Maldivians as Moustri Mili and is buried on Malé.

1761.

Another assault by the fleet of the Ali Raja which was beaten off by a brave attack using 'dhonis'. Again in 1771 the Ali Raja returned determined to conquer the country but was sent off in retreat by the Sultan, Muhammad Ghiyasuddin, who bombarded the pirate ships with a new mortar bought from the Dutch East India Company.

1818 & 1819.

A great famine occurred all over the islands and a massive tornado struck, devasting many islands, homes and boats.

Top, left: Intricate carving of palace roof on Utheemu.

Top, right: The cowrie shell was once the dominant currency of the Indian Ocean countries. It was formerly collected in hundreds of thousands from the lagoons and exported by the boatload.

Left: below: Partly excavated Buddhist mound on Nilandhoo island. Over 80 islands have remains from the Buddhist era.

Right: The last cowrie shop in Malé. The shells have little value today and are exported to India for the souvenir trade.

1835.

The first survey of the islands was undertaken by the British Admiralty under the command of Robert Moresby.

1887.

The Maldives and Great Britain signed an agreement which gave the country the status of a "Protected State".

1932.

The first written Constitution of the Maldives proclaimed.

1953.

First Republic declared.

1953.

Republic dissolved and the Sultanate re-established.

1965.

End of British agreement. Independence and entry into the United Nations.

1968.

Declaration of second Republic.

1976.

British complete withdrawal of all forces from the south of the country.

 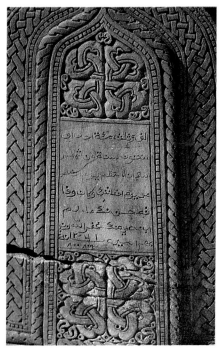 

Left: Remains of a very ancient mosque in the central atolls.

Above, left and right:: Examples of the superb carved grave stones produced over the last eight hundred years by master craftsmen. The Maldivians were famous for their skill in carving these stones. Pointed stones indicate a male is buried there and round ones a female.

Island Life

INTRODUCTION

With somewhere between 1,190 and 2,000 islands within the territorial limits of the Maldives, it is obviously a nation of small islands. Out of these hundreds of islands only 200 are inhabitated, but this number is never constant as over a period of years some islands might be abandoned, whilst others are newly settled. Some islands might be deserted because of large scale erosion.

Although tourism has been present for more than ten years now, its effect on the outer islands has been negligible and on very few islands is there any sign of change brought about through the influence of tourism. A number of fishermen now also catch turtles to supply the lucrative trade in souvenirs which has sprung up in recent years, but the turtle population has become so depleted in the years since the Second World War that this trade is likely to die out very shortly. Some islands, like Hulhudheli, have become somewhat dependent on the tourist trade, abandoning the traditional pursuits of fishing and coconut farming to produce souvenirs from a variety of natural materials for the tourists. However on the majority of islands life is much as it has been for the last few hundred years, the only radical differences perhaps being the introduction of communication facilities allowing rapid contact between islands, atolls and with the administrative capital in Malé — and the introduction of the diesel motor giving the islanders a mobility which they never had with the sail. Education and medical facilities are now also reaching the remote islands.

It is only in recent years that tourism has edged its way up to challenge fishing as the number one foreign currency earner, but this hardly affects the day to day life of the islanders apart from bringing them into contact with increased medical care programmes, and in recent years rapid advancement in the level of schooling available to the children on remote islands.

Some of the sparsely inhabited smaller islands still have no direct contact with the

Left: Fishing 'dhoni' returning to its island before the sun sets.

Above, left: Palm trees dominate the island fauna and are known as the 'tree of life' by the islanders.

Above, right: Mat-weaving. Another of the skills of the women.

outside world and it is very difficult for Europeans to appreciate that these people have never seen many of the things which we take for granted as part of our daily lives. Perhaps they have glimpsed an aeroplane winging its way 30,000 feet above their island, but it is impossible for them to relate this to their life. The remoter islands of the Maldives must be one of the few places left in the entire world where it is possible to find people who have so little contact with Europeans that the children will run, screaming to hide themselves at the sight of a stranger.

There are radical differences in the economies and the lifestyles of different islands up and down the archipelago. Some areas, for instance, might depend solely on fishing for their livelihood, whilst other areas of the Maldives have limited fishing stocks and the islanders need to develop alternative means of survival. This could be the planting of vegetables or fruit crops to take advantage of the south west monsoon which brings heavier rainfall or the production of highly specialised craftwork.

Left, top: The islands of the Maldives are remote communities that have seen very little change over the years.

Left, bottom: Young coconuts awaiting planting.

Above, This fisherman has a slightly unusual catch...two crayfish which he will probably sell to a tourist resort as the flesh is not thought well of by the islanders.

Right: Smashing the sea-soaked coconuts to extract the copra is hard work.

ECONOMY OF THE ISLANDS

The two most important items to the Maldivian islanders are fish and coconuts. These two natural products are the corner stone of island life and almost everything that happens on the islands has a connection to them.

In former times the fishing and coconut industries were of even more importance and Maldivian dried fish and coir rope were the basis of the economy, being exported to countries all over the world. Coir rope is still produced in quantity using the traditional method but it is only for internal use.

The coconut husk is left in the shallows for anything from two weeks to a month and then is pounded by the women for hours in backbreaking work until the fibre strands become separated. The fibres are dried in the sun and then further separated by hand, finally the strands are worked by hand to form ropes of varying thickness. At one time

Left, top: Typical fishing 'dhonis' at anchor.

Bottom, far left: Behind the 'dhonis' are the traditional boat-building huts.

Left: On longer trips the fishermen live on their boats. This 'dhoni' has fire-wood loaded for the trip home and to barter.

Above right: Most large islands have a carpenter, the craft is passed down from father to son.

This page, right: The children start fishing for fun but they soon learn the importance of fish in an environment where there are no alternatives.

this rope from the Maldives was considered to be the best in the world for use on sailing ships and was much sought after by merchants from Arabia, China and Europe.

Cadjan mats from the Maldives were also a trade item a hundred years ago, but like coir it is now mostly produced for use on the islands. The large coconut leaves are woven together using coir rope and these mats are than used as roofing panels or to construct fences marking the boundaries of properties.

The timber from the coconut tree is used in the making of the locally built boats, dhonis, though these days a certain amount of imported timber is used. These seaworthy little craft are built by master carpenters using very few tools or plans but a great deal of skill passed down from generation to generation amongst the same families.

These boats are built in coconut thatched huts at the water's edge and on some islands this forms the economy of the island. Boat carpenters are known as 'kissaru vadin' which means curved carpenters and they command not only a high wage for their efforts but also the respect of the community. It might take only two months for one of these master craftsmen to finish a twelve metre boat using only an axe, adze, drill with wooden handle and iron bit, chisel, mallet and hammer. Domestic carpenters are known as 'ted-ui- vadan' and generally there is one on every inhabited island turning out tables and swings.

The obvious dietary uses of the coconut are well known. The young tender coconuts are known as 'Kurumba' in the Maldives and have a superb sweetness. It is traditional on all the islands for visitors to sit down and quench their thirst with these delicious young coconuts before introductions are commenced. Toddy, known as 'raa,' is a very sweet drink produced by tapping the tree allowing the sap to drip slowly out into containers. Trees used in the production of toddy are not able to produce coconuts and are always marked with the owner's numbers. The sweet drink is popular at special times.

Vinegar is also produced from the coconut, a process that takes about forty days, as is a form of honey known as 'dhiyaa hakuru' which is a derivative of the toddy drink.

From the roots right to the crown the Maldivians have found a use for this tree and it is quite rightly known as the tree of life or more correctly the 'Tree of the Maldives' by the people, and without it in the remoter islands life would be unthinkable. Even today, amongst the changes that are coming with the introduction of tourism and an upswing in the economy, islands are still rented out according to the number of coconut trees present on them.

Until very recently there had been no attempt at plantation farming of coconut, the trees simply growing where the seeds fell, but the government is attempting to introduce management techniques which will eventually lead to more regimented coconut groves. Each tree is known to its owner and it is illegal for visitors to interfere with these plantations without the permission of the owner. Very often it is the case that an inhabited island has an uninhabited island as a neighbour and it is on this island that the coconuts are planted and looked after by a caretaker, owing to a lack of space on the inhabited island allowing only limited agriculture.

Fishing is still the backbone of the Maldivian economy even though challenged today

as the major currency earner by tourism. However tourism might supply the hard currency, but it does not supply the basic economic needs of the islanders. Since time immemorial the sea has done this and with an almost total lack of alternative livestock, apart from poultry which is rare enough to be only used at times of celebration, the importance of fish to the islanders cannot be underestimated.

There are as many fishing methods as there are fish in the ocean, but the most important fish to the Maldivians is without doubt the tuna, as it forms the largest catch at all times of the year. The manner of fishing this abundant creature has changed little in hundreds of years apart from the additional speed given by the introduction of the diesel motor. Much progress has been made in recent years with the introduction of fish gathering devices and large freezer ships which tour the islands.

Fishing is very much a community affair on the islands and follows quite strict procedures over ownership of the boats and the catch. For instance the owner of the boat, or 'masdhoni,' receives the largest portion of the catch, anywhere between 20% and 35% and he may also take one fish per member of the crew in payment for prayers being made for the safety of the crew whilst at sea, though this varies from island to island. The

Left, top: Fishing for the essential bait-fish in the shallow waters of the lagoon. Fishing is very much a community business.

Left: Smaller 'dhoni' setting sail across the lagoon.

Above right: The children's playground is the sea.

remainder of the catch is shared amongst the crew with the chief fisherman, 'Keolu,' receiving most and the chief bait fisherman 'En Keolu,' next in line. Shares in the catch are also given to suppliers on the island for providing such equipment as sails, nets and hooks.

Before setting out for the open sea the fishermen have to catch their bait-fish in the shallows and around the reefs and this means a very early start, well before sunrise.

Once out to sea the fishermen look out for large groups of birds circling, a sure sign of tuna swarming as the terns and noddies know far better than anyone else where the best fishing is to be found. Once the fish have been located the chief fisherman proceeds to throw out the live-bait to attract the tuna, and two men sit on the stern splashing the water vigorously which has the effect of inducing a feeding frenzy amongst the tuna. The bait fish are kept alive in a special compartment of the 'dhoni,' which is flooded with sea-water and this can appear to someone not used to the method as if the boat is sinking. While the men on the stern are splashing the water, four or five others deftly hook the tuna with great skill and in a single motion flip the large fish back into the dhoni and then hook yet another. Although the fishing method might appear to be somewhat primitive it is very effective with as many as a

hundred fish being caught in an hour per person. A twelve hour day is not unusual for these fishermen, who often arrive back to their islands well after dark, where they are eagerly awaited by the other islanders anxious to purchase part of the catch. The fish is normally sold at once on the beach though these days the fishermen usually make a rendezvous with one of the many factory

ships that tour the atolls and sell off most of their catch before returning to the island.

On some islands with a small lagoon surrounded on three sides by land, the villagers have developed a unique manner of fishing for bait-fish and the larger 'fanihandi' which pursue them. These 'fanihandi' are large aggressive fish, commonly known as Trevally, and are a much sought-after delicacy because of their rich white flesh. Very early in the morning, before the sun has risen, the whole village is awake and down on the shoreline at the lagoon. Some people arm themselves with large nets which are used to scoop the bait-fish out of the water whilst others have hand fishing lines. Still others keep a sharp watch on the movements of the swarms of bait-fish in the shallows which swim back and forth in obvious agitation as they know fully well what is coming at them from the reef area. In a sudden explosion of movement and sound the millions of tiny bait fish leap out of the water, in many cases straight into the nets held by the islanders, and just beneath the surface can be seen the sleek deadly forms of the predatory 'fanihandi' as they rip into the massed fish. The men with lines quickly throw them out, baited with a small fish, and in the general confusion the 'fanihandi' is fooled and hooked.

Over the years the Maldivians have not only become master fishermen but also masters at preparing and cooking the fish in a variety of ways. Smoked and sun dried fish, known as 'hiki mas,' is popular with fishermen and travellers, as the flesh keeps for years, and this product still forms an important part of the economy of many islands. In the last century, and even in this century, dried fish was a major export item to India and Sri Lanka and ships would call at the Maldives to take on large quantities of this long-lasting nutrious item. On many islands a large cleared area is kept in the centre of the village for the specific purpose of sun-drying the fish.

Other popular methods of preparing fish are 'fihunu mas', barbecued fish; 'garudhiya' a fish soup; 'gula', fried fish ball with a coating of flour, 'kuli boakiba', spicy fish cake, and finally 'rihaakuru', a paste of high protein content made by boiling fish soup over a long period of time.

The oil from fish also serves the very important task of adding further waterproofing to the hulls of the 'mas dhonis' fishing boats.

Even before the days of tourism the production of hand crafted items from natural materials was a significant part of the economy of individual islands and for the economy as a whole, but with the advent of tourism this small industry has assumed an even greater role in the life of the islanders.

Left, top: Smashing the sea-soaked coconuts to extract the copra is hard work.

Bottom: Dried fish, a major export item of the island.

Right: Lacquer work jar, showing the high level of craftsmanship achieved by the Maldivians using the simplest of tools and materials.

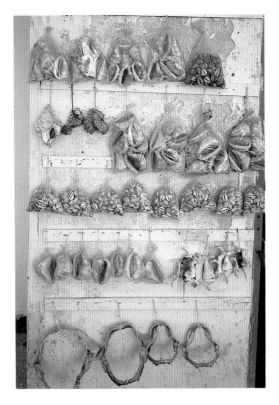

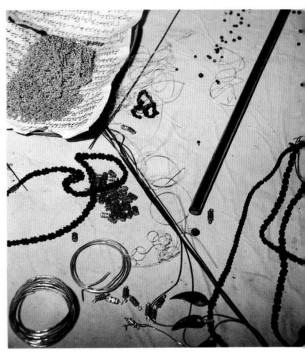

more Maldivian families adopt this lucrative cottage industry it is bound to have some effect on the fragile reef systems of the Maldives.

Other local cottage industries are the production of beautifully woven mats, 'tundu kuna'. The Pandanus leaf is used for weaving baskets. Shells are collected, not only for the tourist trade but also for export to India where they are used in the making of jewellery.

At one time shells were the major export of the Maldives and in particular one small shell played a significant role in the development of the Maldives. This was the cowrie shell known as the money cowrie (Cypraea moneta) which can be found from East Africa to the Galapagos but is particularly abundant in the Maldives.

In the 12th Century the Maldives enjoyed a virtual monopoly of the trade in cowries and found itself one of the richest countries in the world by the simple act of throwing coconut leaves into the water to which the small shells attached themselves. The shells

were then exported by the boatload. At one time as many as forty ships left Malé laden with cowries, and the value in Central Africa was as much as one gold dinar for as few as 1150 cowries. Today the money cowrie has little value apart from being a curiosity.

Agriculture, apart from the coconut, plays a very minor, although essential part in the economy of the islands. Soil cover is so thin on most islands that it is not possible to cultivate long term crops and most agricultural development is confined to seasonal small crops of chillies, tomatoes and fruit crops such as pomegranate, mango, papaya and banana. The southern atolls have a far richer soil and heavier rainfall and are much more fertile than their northern counterparts

In the atoll of Maalhosmadulu Dhekunuburi, particularly on the islands of Thulhaadhoo and Fehen, there are many skilled workers in the production of superb lacquer-work items, which command very high prices representing as they do many hours of professional hand work. Once a year the government holds an exhibition of their work, and some of the pots and boxes reach astonishing standards of craftmanship.

The Maldives has always been well known for its high quality gold and silversmiths and this trade, at one time, often used the treasure from wrecked ships on the reefs to make the jewellery. Today the raw materials are imported but the jewellery is still as fine as in the old days. On certain islands, such as Rimbudu and Huludeli, Nilandhe Dhekunuburi Atoll, whole families are engaged in this cottage industry and have completely abandoned the more traditional pursuits. The fathers and sons collect the raw materials, in the case of black coral and mother of pearl and other shells, diving to great depths without equipment to harvest the coral and shells from the reefs, and fishing with harpoons off the reef for turtles. The women and younger children are employed in grinding down the shells and corals to impart the shine and lustre required, while the older men set the corals and shells in silver and gold surrounds. Some of this hand crafted work reaches an astonishing standard and in particular the bejewelled traditional daggers made from mother-of-pearl are superb, as are also the miniature 'dhonis' made from various shells. As yet this industry has been of a minor nature without a disturbing effect on the environment but as the tourist industry expands from year to year and more and

Left, top: On some islands the people have given up the more traditional pursuits and have started cottage industries producing souvenirs from a range of natural materials. This man is working with turtle shell.

Left, bottom: The whole family works at producing souvenirs for the tourist trade.

Right, top: So far, the trade in souvenirs has not damaged the environment, but as the number of tourists increases year by year the risk also increases.

Right, bottom: Silver and black coral are worked together to make outstanding jewellery.

Left, top: The capital, Malé, from the air. The golden dome of the new Friday mosque can be clearly seen.

Bottom: The Islamic Centre and its great mosque at night. A fitting tribute to the faith of the people.

Right, top: The fish market is often full to overflowing.

Bottom, right: Marine Drive. The road that circles the capital island.

MALÉ: THE ISLAND CAPITAL

In great contrast to the other islands of the Maldives, Malé is a cosmopolitan, modern capital alive with activity almost twenty-four hours a day. But Malé has not always been the capital of the Maldives. Before the coming of Islam, when the islands were first colonised by Aryans from Sri Lanka, the island of Rasgetimu (Maalhosmadulu Uthuruburi atoll) was the captial. Rasgetimu means Kings island in Dhivehi and it was on this island that the Sri Lankan prince, known as Koimala Kalo, was said to have been proclaimed the first King of the Maldives. At this time, or perhaps a bit later, the island of Gaafaru (Malé atoll) was also of great importance, if not the capital. However this first King moved with his retinue to the present island of Malé, soon after assuming the throne and since that day Malé has been the capital.

Malé is the centre of almost all government activity, with the majority of the country's ministries and educational facilities located in its narrow confines, and it is also the communications centre with international and inter-atoll radio communications systems. It is the home of the Citizens Majlis where representatives from the capital and outer islands meet regularly to discuss legislation and other matters.

With almost 60,000 people crammed into

This page, top: The Islamic Centre by day.

Bottom: Malé is the centre for education, although many schools have now been built on the remoter atolls.

Opposite page, top: A clear sign of the Maldivians pride in their independance.

Centre, left: Wood is precious on the remoter islands where it is often the only source of fuel for cooking. The capital island has a busy wood-market.

Centre, right: Colourful example of the unique Maldivian language, 'Dhivehi'.

Bottom: Bananas are grown on many of the outer islands and brought to Malé to be sold.

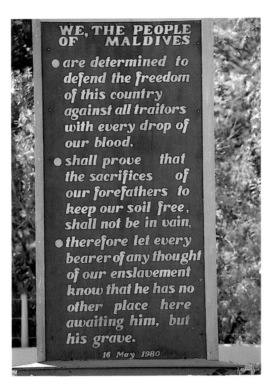

WE, THE PEOPLE
OF MALDIVES

- are determined to defend the freedom of this country against all traitors with every drop of our blood,
- shall prove that the sacrifices of our forefathers to keep our soil free, shall not be in vain,
- therefore let every bearer of any thought of our enslavement know that he has no other place here awaiting him, but his grave.

16 May 1980

a two square mile area, Malé still manages to retain an aura of calm where business and leisure are carried out in a relaxed manner suitable to the hot climate. Even though the population of Malé has grown nearly ten times since 1921 when a census revealed a population of 6,127, the island does not give the impression of being overcrowded. On the contrary it is possible to wander around the small back streets and meet with very few people. Much of the new population of Malé is transient, living on boats in the crowded harbour or staying for a few weeks with relatives. It is the custom for islanders to visit Malé for a few months, find work and earn enough money to raise the stakes to join a community venture to build a new fishing boat, then return to their island.

Viewed from the sea, Malé has altered its appearance over the last two hundred years or so with large scale land reclamation projects having enlarged the area of the island and altered its shape. The old fort and sea walls have gone to be replaced by the modern harbour and the skyline is now dominated by the splendid golden dome of the new Islamic centre, known as Masjid Al-Sultan Mohammad Thakurufaan Al-A"Z'am which was completed in November 1984. This large building is a fitting tribute to the faith of the people, which has endured for almost a thousand years, and houses an Islamic library, education centre as well as the Grand Mosque. Friday sees almost the entire male population of Malé at midday prayer and the Grand Mosque becomes so full that many have to stand on the steps outside. There is a special area inside the Grand Mosque for women to pray, as well as in other mosques scattered around the capital.

A few modern government buildings now also dominate the skyline of Malé, but most houses and shops are no higher than two storeys. The old bazaar area is still the centre of commerce with hundreds of tiny shops lining the narrow streets selling everything from fish hooks to diesel engines. Many of the shops still sell local products from the outer islands, but with tourism has come an obvious trend to stock more luxury goods and the number of souvenir shops that have sprung up in recent years is quite phenomenal. This busy area directly behind the main 'dhoni' harbour is also the site for the colourful, busy markets. The fish market is the largest but for much of the day deserted until the fishing 'dhonis' start to arrive in the evening when the market is transformed into the busiest place in the Maldives. Individual buyers looking for something for that night's dinner are joined by traders looking for bargains to supply hotels and tourist islands and the competition can be fierce. Outside the

market are queues of the old carts still used by many to deliver fresh fish to the hotels and private houses. Some of the fish never actually reach the market, for as soon as the boats draw up to the harbour people are waiting to buy the fish directly from the fishermen.

Directly next to the fish market is the wood market which has a much more casual atmosphere as wood, unlike fish, is not perishable and the sellers are in no great hurry to dispose of their wares and can afford to hold out for better prices.

The fruit and vegetable market is under cover and open till late in the night and has a very exotic atmosphere with its pungent odour of tropical fruits. Everything that the islanders can grow or import is on sale. Bananas hang from the ceiling in bunches which are bought by islanders making a long voyage back home. The bananas can be tied to a mast and eaten as they slowly mature. Pineapples, papaya, mangos, watermelons, limes, small local oranges, chillies, sweet potatoes and many other fruits and vege-

Far left: The 'Medhu Ziyaarath'. The tomb of the Islamic missionary, Abul Barakaath Yoosuf Al Barbary who first brought Islam to the Maldives in 1153 AD.

Top: The harbour is always busy with the arrival of passenger and cargo 'dhonis' and the return of the fisherman in the afternoon is the high point of everyday.

Bottom, left: The area behind the fish market is full of colourful shops selling everything from fish hooks to diesel motors.

Bottom, right: Timeless atmosphere of the fruit and vegetable market on Malé.

tables are all on sale but without a doubt the most popular items are the betel nuts and leaves. These two locally grown products are used by Maldivians to indulge a favourite

Left, top: The Friday mosque.

Bottom: The tomb of the Maldivian hero, Muhammad Thakurufaan, who defeated the Portugese in 1573 and regained the nation's sovereignty.

Above: Entrance to the 'Medhu Ziyaarath' showing the distinctive Islamic architecture and design.

Right: The minaret of the Friday mosque.

habit present throughout most of the Indian subcontinent. The betel nut is sliced and wrapped in the leaf along with a small amount of coral lime and a stick of clove. This mixture is then chewed at leisure by the Maldivians. The juice from the betel nut produces a bright red colour and many of the older people have teeth and gums permanently stained from this habit. Locally made cigarettes known as 'bidis' are smoked while enjoying the betel nut and these are single leaves of tobacco rolled up in old newspapers and have a strength that will leave others gasping for breath. All around the market area are small stalls set up by men and women selling these ready made cigarettes and sliced betel nuts and no self-respecting Maldivian fisherman would ever leave port without his little box containing bidis, betel nut, leaves and the lime powder.

Malé has many historical and religious sites of great importance and the most important monument must be the original Friday Mosque,'Hukuru Miskiy,' perhaps the third oldest mosque in the Maldives, but more important as the centre for Islam for many hundred years and because of its wealth of inscriptions which provide various clues to the history of the country. In its confines are buried many of the famous men of Maldivian history, Sultans and wise men.

The carvings on the actual building and some of the surrounding crypts reach a superb standard and it is easy to see why the Maldivians were much sought after as stone carvers in earlier times. Hidden away in the back streets, not far from the Friday Mosque, is the site of the oldest mosque in the Maldives, built in the year 1153 AD when Sultan Muhammad ul-Adil embraced the Islamic faith. The small memorial and grave of the Maldivian hero, Muhammad Thakurufaanu, is located a small distance away in the back streets.

With the economic benefits that the emerging tourist industry has brought, the capital is undergoing many changes. New schools, improved hospital facilities and modern government buildings are signs of the changing times and the rapid improvement in the living standards of the people.

The opening of the International Airport on the nearby island of Hulule in 1981 has influenced Malé a great deal, and where twenty years ago the capital was really one of the remotest locations in the world, today it is the vibrant centre of a rapidly expanding country with internatonal airlines like Singapore Airlines making ten flights a week and charter flights from Europe arriving daily.

Much is also changing in the character of Malé; where once only carts trundled around the narrow streets it is not unusual to see large motor cars and powerful motorbikes. But still much is as it was, though with the population increasing and tourism expanding on almost a daily basis change is inevitable.

THE OUTER ISLANDS

Travelling from north to south over the entire Maldives the islands, almost without exception, are much the same. All are of a small size with the surrounding reef breached in a few places by the islanders to allow the passage of boats. On the sea side, the beach tends to be rough with a narrow area between reef and shore, while on the leeward side there is a wide shallow lagoon protecting the sandy beach. Very often it is possible for the fishermen to beach their craft on the deeply shelving shore. This is particularly common in the northern atolls but in the central and southern atolls the lagoons tend to be so narrow that boats have to be left far out on the reef edge and small boats used to transport supplies and people to the shoreline. From a distance the islands appear to be heavily covered by dense growth but on closer inspection this is revealed to be plantations of coconuts which are not as thick as first impressions convey. Almost always, running directly through the middle of the island most often at cross angles to the beach entrance, is a wide boulevard stretching from one beach to another. Centred around the boulevard is the village, which apart from the large central track has narrow streets running off to all points of the island.

Walls made from coral line the narrow streets to a height of an average Maldivian. This is because bathing facilities are located outside and the walls are there to ensure privacy as well as to mark boundaries. Surrounded by a verdant and fertile garden, the small houses are also built from coral blocks. The 'cement' used in the construction is obtained locally by burning coral slowly in deep pits which ultimately yields a powerful lime adequate for building purposes. Simple cadjan thatched coconut leaves are used for roofing though these are slowly but surely being replaced by corrugated sheeting which lacks the natural feel of the cadjan.

Generally speaking the rooms of the house are tiny, few in number and dark, though the ceiling is high to aid heat circulation. Furniture is minimal and usually confined to a rudimentary flat wooden bench which serves as a bed at night and a sitting place during the day. There might be a few pictures on the wall showing some of the holy sites of Islam and many houses boast an old clock, which has pride of place. Tucked under the bed-cum-sofa is a heavy wooden chest where the family valuables and heirlooms are kept. The lack of furniture denotes that most activity takes place outside and it is certainly more comfortable in such a climate. To sit under the shade of one of the massive bread-fruit trees where it is always possible to find a breeze blowing in from the sea. Under the shade of these trees and often on the small verandah that every house has, is the 'undoali,' a large wooden swing which

is also a great aid to cooling down when no fans or winds are available. There are also the hammock-type chairs made from wood and coir rope which are known as 'joali.'

The kitchen is never located in the house but in the garden and is even more rudimentary than the living quarters being normally open on all sides except one. Cooking facilities are sparse as electricity or gas is not available and the islanders use what they have done for hundreds of years, an open wooden fire. Wood is a precious commodity in the Maldives, so precious that the capital Malé has a large market specially devoted to the sale and barter of firewood. The women

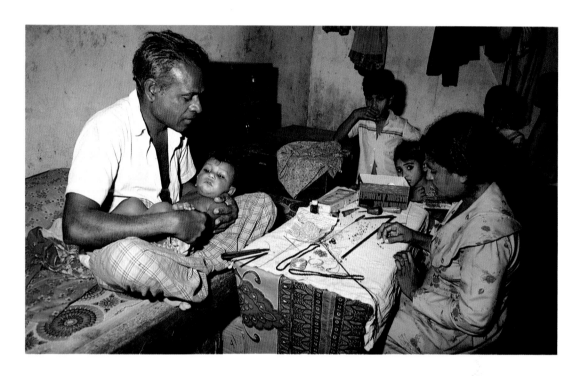

Left : This retired
fisherman takes a month
to produce one hand
crafted knife.

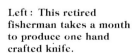

Above, right: The whole
family joins in the trade
of this father. He is a
silversmith of some
fame in the islands and
his family has been
producing jewellery for
centuries.

Bottom right: Three
Months careful work has
gone into this mother of
pearl model of a
'Dhoni'.

are able to collect some firewood fuel from their own island in the natural course of clearing vegetation for planting, but great care has to be exercised as over-collecting on an inhabited island can lead to large scale erosion which in itself can cause the island to be abandoned when there is not enough soil to sustain crops. So the normal method of collecting firewood is to visit a nearby uninhabited island once a month or so by boat, but even this has to be managed with care. Firewood is also exchanged for fish, vegetables or fruits.

The majority of households have a well sunk to a depth of about two metres and this taps the rain water reservoirs that are under most islands. Water is drawn from the 'gifili' with the aid of a long wooden pole on the end of which is a large tin called 'dhaani.' People unused to the system experience great difficulty in manipulating this device, with more water ending up on the earth than over the body. Drinking water is nowadays most often obtained from modern storage tanks built by the government next to the village mosque. Recently the islanders started constructing water tanks which collect the rainfall during the monsoons.

The women of the islands shoulder a large burden of the day-to-day work whilst the men are out fishing or tending the coconut plantations. As has already been mentioned they are responsible for the collection of firewood and

Left, top: Traditional coral built houses with thatched roofs.

Bottom: Most houses have a wall-lined garden.

Right: Perhaps the best smile in the world is to be found on a young Maldivian girl.

clearing vegetation to make way for crop planting but they also perform many other tasks. Perhaps the most back-breaking work they do is the preparation of the raw coconut fibre for the making of coir rope, but the task of collecting the fine coral from the beaches and then hauling it back to the village in baskets on the head is also exacting. The coral is used to resurface the floors of the house and surrounding garden area and is put down regularly. A communal use of this soft white coral is to remake the road running through the centre of the island. Everyday a group of women brush the coral. One of the most pleasing aspects of the Maldives, is that everything is always spotless, and no

effort is spared by the villagers in ensuring that, not only their own house, but the whole island is kept clean.

The simple domestic chores for the women of the Maldives are time consuming and difficult given the facilities and commodities that are available. Without the possibilities of cold storage for foodstuffs everything has to be prepared fresh daily and perishable items such as milk, butter, meat and fresh vegetables are generally not available. The staple food items are fish and rice, though a flat bread is prepared by grating coconut flesh and mixing it with flour then baking it on a thin sheet of tin over an open fire. To the fish might be added precious limes and chillies as well as grated coconut to produce an acceptable curry that is normal breakfast fare. For the evening fish again, but this time as a thin soup to soak into the rice. A common sight during the day is women sitting in the garden with a large flat pan full of rice from which they carefully pick out and discard the black seeds and other paddy

Left, top: Girls sifting coral in the early morning.

Bottom, left: The fine coral is taken back to the house and used to recover the floors.

Bottom, right: The women work hard the whole day and at the same time bring up a bevy of children. These women are dressed in the traditional manner of the islanders.

Right: This sleeping child sums up the peaceful atmosphere of the remoter islands.

Top, right: Not much time for play and leisure but the Maldivians enjoy such games as 'carrom'.

husks. This is a time when many of the women exchange gossip under the shade of the trees on the ever present swing.

On special occasions, like the circumcision ceremony, delicacies will be prepared by the women and even one of the precious chickens slaughtered to make a delicious curry. Spicy fish cakes 'kuli boakiba,' fried fish balls 'gula,' and sweet pastry pudding

'foni boakiba,' will be cooked along with a sweet drink known as 'kiru sarbat.'

The girls marry very early, usually around the 15th or 16th year and it is not uncommon for the women to have many children before they are out of their teens. Divorce rates are very high and it is not unusual to find a woman who has been married four or five times.

The wedding ceremony is usually conducted in the boy's house, though sometimes in the island office. Once the boy has the agreement of the girl he intends to wed he informs the Gazi (local judge) who then arranges to meet the girl and confirm what the boy has told him. The girl, at this time, must inform the Gazi how much the 'ran' is. This is a nominal payment that the groom makes to the bride, very often not more than a few dollars, which is given over to the girl's guardian. The wedding is a very minor affair which the bride does not usually attend, only the groom, two witnesses and the Gazi need be there. Strict records are kept on all

islands of weddings. There is hardly ever a celebration afterwards though these days a small tea-party might be held. Like many Islamic countries a great deal of fuss is not made of family life or connections and this can appear somewhat strange to a Westerner, unused to the Maldivian way. For instance a son who has not seen his mother for a few years will not react with a great deal of emotion at a meeting nor vice versa and this lack of obvious emotion is also very noticeable in the Maldivian language, Dhivehi. There are no formal greetings in the language, few expressions of concern and certainly no words exist for 'thank you' and 'please'.

It is important to note however that the Dhivehi langauge has a complex system of levels and a person addressing another may use a level of language that in itself implies the courtesy and politeness required without using actual words for this.

Islam is such an integral part of life in the islands of the Maldives that there is no dividing line between religion and other aspects of daily life. At the centre of even the smallest

Left, top: Many islands are unapproachable by the larger boats and smaller boats ferry goods and passengers out to them.

Bottom, left: The traditional house built in front of the landing area where visitors are greeted and important matters discussed by islanders.

Bottom, right: Children at play. Behind them is a poster warning of the dangers of polluting the environment.

Right: Islam is the cornerstone of life in the Maldives. This old man spends his entire day sitting in the mosque and reciting the Koran.

village is the mosque, or 'miskiy' as it is known locally. Some uninhabited islands boast mosques and on islands where only a single caretaker is resident he will have constructed a makeshift mosque from coconut leaves and wood. The mosque is not only at the geographical centre of the village it also is the centre of village life, where at prayer times the villagers come together to face Mecca and pay obediance to a religion that is the very core of their life. From the time they are born to the time they die, Islam embraces them in an all encompassing manner and gives the islanders a consistency which their lives would perhaps otherwise lack.

Many of the mosques are ancient structures and it is not uncommon for these to have been built on the foundations of old Buddhist temples which gives them an antiquity lost in the mist of time. In many of the mosques are exquisite wood carvings in Arabic matched with superb lacquer work pillars and roof panels.

Where modern schooling is not available — though more and more islands have new schools as part of the governments drive for education for all — most children are educated by an 'edurube,' an Islamic teacher who will teach the children to read the Arabic alphabet and eventually the Koran. This form of schooling has not changed in almost a thousand years and the children can still be seen making their way to the small schools clutching their slate boards on which they write out the Arabic words.

Every island has a certain number of boats at its disposal, even if they are only open fishing boats, and these are used to take produce to market in Malé. All the islands are dependent on the capital for supplies and foodstuffs which they are unable to produce themselves. Again it is organised on a community basis with the fishing boats being laden with produce from all the islanders — vegetables or precious fruits, coconuts, dried fish, wood and various other commodities. All are taken by some of the men to sell or barter in the markets in Malé. The produce is sold or exchanged for rice, poultry, eggs,

Left, top: Smaller passenger 'dhoni' unloading cargo in the far north.

Bottom, left: Loading fire-wood onto a cargo boat at sea.

Bottom, right: One of the larger passenger and cargo boats that ply the atoll routes and at times even venture as far afield as Sri Lanka or India.

Above, right: The modern Islamic school and study centre built on the island of Utheemu in memory of Muhammad Thakurufaan.

Left: 'Bodu beru'
is a unique dance form
to the Maldives. Its
origins are obscure and
the dancing can become
so intense that men fall
into a trance-like state.

Top, centre: 'Raivaru'
is the almost
dead art of reciting
poetry. This old man is
considered a master of
the art and performs a
slow dance while reciting.
Much of what he says is
in such an old form of
the language that the
younger generation
cannot understand it.

Above, right: Very few
sun-dials remain, but at
one time the 'call to
pray' was measured by
this alone.

cigarettes and items of luxury, like tinned milk and soft drinks. Very often there is a small shop on each island and this supplies basic food items like rice and flour and also hardware needed for construction purposes and equipment for fishing.

As well as the island boats, 'dhonis' call at the major islands and their arrival is always greeted with excitement with the whole village turning out to see who is arriving and what goods are for sale These are locally built boats of a considerable size carrying as many as 200 passengers and much cargo, but not in what might be termed comfort. They are seaworthy craft able to withstand the worst monsoon storms of the region but roll about in a sickening motion because of their curious construction which is very top-heavy with superstructure thrown on without design or forethought. Some of these craft often make the journey to India or Sri Lanka which proves their capabilities. Smaller islands are not visited by such boats and the islanders can experience great problems if they wish to travel to another island or the capital. They have to island-hop from one to another in small boats until they reach a larger island which is a stop for the 'dhonis'. An inter-island transport project is underway and should give the islanders more mobility in the future.

There is not a great deal of time for leisure on the islands but what little time there is, is used by the islanders to enjoy simple games. Adults rarely have time for any leisure so most games are played by the children. Sports are popular and even the smallest island has a football pitch and inter-island matches, especially in Malé, are keenly followed by much of the population. Badminton, cricket and volleyball are also very popular and Maldivians excell particularly at volleyball.

Chess is played everywhere with slightly different rules from the Western style. The traditional board game is 'carrom,' an Arabic board game played with small round wooden pieces which are shoved over an ornate board in a manner not dissimilar to billiards without the cue. A board game from the Maldives, but probably introduced from Africa hundred of years ago, is 'ovvalu' which is played with money cowries on a carved wooden base with 16 oval depressions. Many children learn their arithmetic by playing this game.

Celebration times are infrequent, birthdays and the like passing without notice as in other Islamic countries. But the period following the religious fasting month of 'Ramazan' is always a time of enjoyment and celebration. This is known as the 'Eid-ul-Fitr' (kuda Id) festival and is a time to prepare and enjoy special sweets and dishes and relax. From sunrise to sunset the Maldivians take no food or water for the month of 'Ramazan'

and this is particularly hard for the fishermen as fish still need to be caught for the evening meals and to sustain the economy in this month. Two months and ten days after this Eid there is the 'Eid-ul-Azha' (Bodu Id), another time for celebration.

'Haiy Dhuvas' is the naming ceremony which occurs on the seventh or fourteenth day after birth. An Arabic name is usually given pertinent to the day, month and year. In the past the father would shave a sliver of hair from the head and a small party would follow.

The circumcision ceremony is perhaps the most extravagant and elaborate one in the Maldives with very often a group of boys undergoing the harmless operation together and the families sharing in the celebrations. A special house is prepared, decked out with colourful paper-streamers and for three or four days loud music blares out as relations and other visitors pay their respects to the families of the young men and enjoy the tasty food especially prepared for the occasion. It is normal for the boys to undergo circumcision at about the age of six or seven and for much of the celebration these boys lie under white sheets stretched out on beds until they feel well enough to join in the fun. This is one of

the occasions when the unique music and dancing of the islands can be seen; villagers gather together with a variety of musical instruments and indulge their passion for song and dance. There are many forms of traditional folk-singing and dancing but the most popular is without a doubt 'Bodu Beru', a heavy and rhythmic form of music played out on homemade drums accompanied by Arabic lyrics and sometimes wild dancing. The Bodu Beru has its origins in both Arabic and African music and like much of Maldivian music, shows the diverse origins and influences of the Maldivian people. The dancing follows a fairly traditional pattern until the music speeds up and then the dancers go into a semi-hypnotic state which leaves them in a trance when the music finally ends.

The women have their own traditional music and this is known as 'bandiya jehun' where they beat out a rhythm on metal water pots while singing and shaking their long hair in time to the music. 'Tara' is another dance and 'raivaru' is a form of reciting poetry and verse in slow song form that is unfortunately dying out. Only the older men remember this art and the words are often expressed in a very old language which few people understand today.

Typical scenes from a Maldivian tourist island.

THE TOURIST ISLANDS

Although this book is not intended as a travel guide to the 50-60 tourist islands in the Maldives, some information is perhaps relevant with the growing importance of this industry.

'Paradise' is a very difficult subject; each man's vision of paradise is radically different from someone else's. But there is no doubt that the majority of visitors to these charming islands take away with them a feeling of having seen one of the last real 'Paradises' left on our overcrowded planet. The majority of the tourist islands are small. There are exceptions like Bandos and Villingili where it is possible to walk entirely round the island in fifteen minutes or less. There are no cars and the only noise that might disturb the peaceful atmosphere is the generator that each island must have to supply the comforts that the tourists expect on an island. The generator is always located at a good distance from the accommodation anyway.

Degree of comfort and facilities vary from island to island; some have five-star ratings and are the equal to similar clubs and islands in other parts of the world, while others are wonderfully primitive with the air-conditioning supplied by a breeze on the beach.

It is a casual relaxed atmosphere on these islands. A chance to really get away from our hectic world, forget about troublesome events and concentrate on important matters like whether the chef will catch a large fish for the barbecue that evening.

The normal type of holiday activities that the European tourists seem to enjoy like discos, night-clubs and fancy-dress parties are very rare. But what there is, more than compensates: a superbly warm tropical sea, pure white beaches with no litter, huge palm trees rustling in a balmy breeze, sunsets and sunrises of a rare beauty and finally the reefs which offer anyone able to swim a chance to join in the greatest show on earth. The underwater world of the Maldives is bursting with life, life and more life. There are two occasions in the Maldives when a first time visitor is left open-mouthed in amazement. The first is when the jet that has brought them from Europe, drops down through the cloud cover of 30,000 feet and the islands are suddenly revealed in all their glory. An unbelievable sight. The second time is when the hesitant swimmer crosses the crown of the reef and suddenly comes face to face with the overwhelming sight of a coral reef for the first time.

Most islands have a diving school, where over a period of two weeks tourists can undergo professional tuition at cheap rates. This is a chance not to be missed as the Maldives really does offer some of the best diving in the world. It is no less a pleasure

just to snorkel and let a slow current glide one along the reef crown at a leisurely rate.

Sailing activities are catching on fast and many islands now have sailboards and small catamarans available for the visitors. Water skiing is quite rare, perhaps a good thing considering the associated noise and pollution not in keeping with the islands' undisturbed atmosphere.

The Maldives is no place for the visitor who arrives with a pack on their back and an idea of travelling around the islands on their own. This is not possible and can turn out to be twice as expensive as booking a package tour in Europe in the first place. The only place to go, without an island reservation, is the capital Malé where accommodation is hard to find. Malé has no beaches whatsoever and even if it did, the sight of scantily clad Europeans wandering around would not be welcome in the capital of this Islamic Republic. Once on Malé the thing to do is visit the nearby tourist islands. This means the hire of a boat for the journey there and back which can prove very expensive and there is always the possibility that the owners of the island will turn away day visitors. Camping and other activities of this nature are completely forbidden. Special permission, not easily obtained, is needed to visit any inhabited island (though trips are made from some tourist resorts to these islands by special arrangement).

There are many boats offering diving or scenic tours around the islands and this is one of the best ways to see the Maldives. A one week trip on such vessels can be an exhilarating and enjoyable experience and very cheap for a group of six or eight people. Most of the boats have diving and sailing equipment, showers and other comforts.

Very few tourists find themselves in ill-health in the Maldives; the sun, simple food and healthy exercise tends to tone up a body that has been suffering in the colder climes of Europe. The recently expanded hospital on Malé is never far away and in the last few years air-ambulances have been operating in and out of the country in emergency cases. With two to three wide-bodied jets touching down everyday, the Maldives is no longer the isolated community it once was and medical care in a crisis is not that far away.

Malaria is unknown — but mosquitos are. Some islands are plagued by the creatures but fortunately most tourist islands have been chosen carefully to avoid this problem. The best preventive measure is to use 'insect-off' lotions which keep the pests well away.

The islands of the Maldives form one of the last natural parts of the world left to us, and all visitors should respect this and not remove living parts of the reef system such as shells and coral. If every tourist took something away with them there would soon be nothing left to amaze anyone else in the future.

Left, top: Launches in the lagoon of a tourist island.

Bottom left and right: If a tourist is looking for peace and 'paradise', they will find it here.

The Flora And Fauna

Islands in the middle of oceans are not noted for their abundant wildlife and the Maldives are no exception, showing a rather restricted albeit interesting flora and fauna. The main interest is in the comparison of island forms as compared to their mainland counterparts, as divergence has bound to have taken place over many thousands of years. Little serious research work has been undertaken into the wildlife of the country, but as interest gains ground in the Maldives about the environment much more should become known and it is expected several new forms of certain species will be discovered.

The flora of the Maldives is surprisingly diverse and the islands by no means have the impoverished plant life that could be imagined considering such a poor soil cover and hostile environment. In the south, islands like Fuamulaku and Hithadhoo are luxuriant in their flora with large freshwater lakes and dense, almost tropical jungle. Most of the fauna has arrived on the archipelago using the Laccadives and the direct drift from the north-easterly monsoon winds and certainly the majority of the wildlife originates from India and Sri Lanka.

The possibilities of colonisation from the direction of Africa should not be discounted however as the fauna of the southern area demonstrates. After careful study it will probably be revealed that the fauna and flora shares just as diverse an origin as the Maldivian people themselves.

The reptilian fauna shows how strong the connection between Sri Lanka and the Maldives is regarding its wildlife as all the species to be found are also found in Sri Lanka. Two nocturnal house geckos are widespread, both *Hemidactylus* species, *frenatus* and *brookii*, (Ho Anu) distinguished by the large unblinking eyes and the adhesive sucker-like tips of the toes which allows them to scale vertical smooth surfaces. Particularly common on some islands is the colourful garden lizard, *Calotes versicolor*, (Bondu). This handsome agamid lizard is often seen scuttling for cover in dense vegetation or up the trunk of a tree. The males are smart with their reddish heads and yellow tails which become more obvious in the breeding season or when two males are having a territorial dispute. The females tend to be a duller colour which serves as good camouflage when they are on the ground.

A fast moving skink is much rarer but can occasionally be seen sunning itself on a wall and this is *Riopa albopunctata*, (garahita). Two types of snake are known to exist and it is likely that even more could be found. Neither of the two are poisonous and they are a species of *Typhlops*, *braminus*, (Nannugathi) and the wolf snake, *Lycodon aulicus capucinus*. The latter lives in holes and dense vegetation where it feeds on the lizards. One frog is known, the short-headed *Rana breviceps*, and a large toad has also been found, *Bufo melanostictus*, (Boh). Old records exist of tortoises once existing on Hulule island, now the international airport, but these must have been introductions.

Left, top & bottom:
Colony of flying foxes.

Right: Agamid lizard.

The smaller members of the animal kingdom in the Maldives are a subject virtually unknown up till now but probably like much of the higher fauna they show the same connections to the nearby mainlands. More than 67 species of butterfly have been identified and there are a few surprises, like the small scorpion, common all over the Maldives, which possesses a strong though not dangerous sting, and the large aggressive centipede which can inflict a nasty bite with its adapted front claws. Paper wasps are seen building their curious nests around buildings and the large armoured rhinocerous beetle is always busy amongst the flowering plants and coconut plantations where it causes considerable damage.

As the Maldives moves into the 21st Century much of its wildlife will come under increasing pressure and it would be tragic if any of the rare forms were to disappear. However the government has shown an increasing awareness and concern for its envi-

ronment and the recent steps of creating a National Environmental Council and sponsoring research and conservation work bodes well for the future.

The majority of birds to be found in the Maldives are sea birds. At first, land birds might appear to be non-existent but closer inspection reveals a surprising variety for such a restricted environment. There are thought to be as many as 113 different species of birds found in the Maldives but out of these less than twenty can be considered as truly resident. However, with further investigation this list is bound to grow.

Resident land birds are not so obvious on the tourist or inhabited islands but on some of the uninhabited islands they can be fairly common. Without a doubt the two most common land birds are the Indian house crow *Corvus splendens*, (Kaalhu) and the Koel bird *Eudynamys scolopacea* (the male is called Kaalhu Koveli and the female Dindin Koveli). These two can be seen on most islands including the capital, Malé, and the tourist islands. On many inhabited islands

Left, top: Large freshwater lake in the south.

Bottom, left: Maldivian little heron.

Bottom, right: The everpresent house crow. A serious pest on many islands.

Above, right: Fresh-water shells.

the house crows have reached pest proportions. It is thought that these crows came with the first colonisers of the islands many years ago, as they were carried by the seafarers in these days to determine the proximity and direction of land. The crows were released when land was thought to be near and if the birds flew off strongly in one direction this indicated that an island was there. However if the crow circled and then returned to the ship no land was nearby. The crows are found everywhere except below the Equatorial channel and have become a thorn in the side of the islanders, taking fish as it is laid out in the sun to dry, stealing valuable young poultry and picking the best of the rare fruits and vegetables before they are fully ripe. Various methods have been tried to control these birds but all have so far failed. Poisoning or shooting has the effect of increasing the population as the decimated birds breed at an even faster rate to take advantage of the increase in food available. Even on uninhabited islands these crows fly immediately out to have a look at any new boat arriving and any activity on the beach by humans is always carefully watched.

The Koel bird is a member of the cuckoo family and like all members of this family it is parasitic, laying its eggs in other birds' nests. The host bird in this case is the house crow and wherever the crow is seen, the Koel is sure to be found. This bird is more often heard than seen particularly early in the morning when it will sit at the top of a tall tree and let forth with some of the most amazing noises to come from a bird. Its repertoire is wide, consisting of what sounds like a young girl screaming or, just as common, a single hoot which is raised up and

Left, top: Black-naped terns in courtship.

Bottom, left: The handsome and elusive fairy tern, confined to islands below the equator.

Bottom, right: Hawksbill turtle. Once a common sight on the reefs.

Right: Herons on freshwater lake in the south.

down the scales. The male and female are quite distinct, the male being all black with the shimmering plumage common to the starling family and distinguished by a bright green bill. The female has a spotted plumage, brown to black in colour.

Surprisingly the common sparrow has a sparse presence on the islands and only populates the capital Malé in small numbers. It

Top, left: Grey heron colony.

Right: Small brown scorpion, common on many islands.

Bottom, left: Maldivian pond heron.

Bottom, right: The large Grey heron.

was said to be introduced some ten years ago but has not really prospered.

The rose-ringed parakeet, *Psittacula krameri*, is a much commoner introduction, being found around Malé and the surrounding islands. In the evenings its distinctive call can be heard anywhere near vegetation and it is the only member of the parrot family to habitate the Maldives. It is easily identified in flight by its long tail feathers, bright green colour and red bill.

The only other land bird to be seen in any numbers is the white breasted waterhen *Amaurornis phoenicurus maldivus*, (Kambili) which contrary to its name is not often found by water in the Maldives but usually in the densely vegetated centre of the islands. This is another bird more often heard than seen and any strange noises emanating from the thick vegetation can be attributed to this waterhen. It breeds during the monsoons and at times can be highly aggressive, chasing away human and other intruders from its nesting area with a loud scolding call. Easily identified by its white breast that is more

pronounced in the male which has a brighter plumage, this bird is classified as a separate race around the Malé atoll and, as such, is one of the unique birds of the Maldive islands in need of further study and most certainly some form of protection. Another shy water bird that has only been recorded a few times is the water cock, *Gallicrex cinerea*, (Hulhi-Kukulhu) which resembles a large moorhen.

At different times of the year it is possible to see a variety of migrants passing through the country, many of them blown off course by strong winds during the monsoons. This list includes birds of prey such as harriers, falcons and even buzzards, but also includes a large number of the wading birds. Seven or more species of plover, the trunstone, snipe, whimbrel, godwit, curlew and sandpipers are all seen during the winter.

The kestrel *Falco tinnunculus*, (Surumuthi), a small bird of prey once thought to be only a visitor is most certainly now resident on some islands, and definitely in Malé atoll where it is seen all year round.

Top: Crab plovers.

Bottom: Terns in flight.

As many as thirteen different types of heron live in the Maldives, without a doubt the commonest being the large Grey heron *Ardea cinerea rectirostris*, (Maakanaa) which is often seen standing like a sentinal on the outer reefs of the islands waiting to spear a fish with its long and sharp bill. This heron breeds throughout the archipelago and no island seems without its resident heron guarding the reef entrance. Three of the smaller herons are thought to be forms unique to the Maldives and these are the central or paler Maldivian little heron *Butorides striatus didii*, (Raabondhi), the southern or darker Maldivian little heron *Butorides striatus albidulus*, (Raabondhi) and the Maldivian pond heron *Ardeola grayii phillipsi*. None of the three is seen often if, at all. All are in need of further study as it would be sad to see these unique forms of Maldivian fauna disappear before action can be taken to ensure their survival.

The true sea birds are the most obvious of Maldivian birds and at least 15 types are breeding residents. Most of these are terns and include the very beautiful and rare white or fairy tern *Gygis alba* (Kandhu-Wallu-Dooni) which is confined to the atoll of Addu. This graceful pure white bird, with its pale blue bill, is the subject of many legends in the atoll and the locals attribute its presence as a key factor for the total lack of the Indian house crow in the atoll. This certainly has some basis of truth as the fairy terns will not tolerate the presence of any dark bird regardless of size. It only needs the appearance of a wandering buzzard or a similar bird to trigger their aggressive behaviour. In an instant the whole sky of Addu is full of these white birds as they swoop through the air in their hundreds diving and screaming at the intruder. They will actually hit the offender and the darker noddy terns are often found dead or with broken wings after a mobbing by the territorial white terns. The people of Addu are fond of this little bird and never disturb it when it is nesting. The terns commonly nest in gardens where they lay their single egg on the branch of a breadfruit-tree and rear the chick without any nest what so ever. Very often children will play with the chicks but the parent birds are not upset and even fly down to the hand to feed the youngster.

Legend has it that this tern was introduced to Addu by a Moslem Saint many hundreds of years ago to drive away the crows which had reached plague proportions. Again this may have an element of truth in it. The fairy tern exists in the Seychelles and even though the terns are strong flyers and could have colonised Addu atoll naturally, it does not explain why they do not appear elsewhere in the Maldives. Yet another mystery in Addu is the occurence of the parasitic Koel bird which is quite common there. One won-

ders how it survives without its host bird, the Indian house crow.

Another bird that has probably colonised the south of the Maldives from the Seychelles is the frigate-bird. Two types occur within the southern islands and these are the great frigate-bird, *Fregata minor* and the lesser frigate-bird, *Fregata ariel*, (hoara). Both are large black birds with long forked tails that are usually seen high overhead gliding over flocks of terns. The frigate birds are master flyers which attack and harry the terns until they drop the fish they have caught. In a remarkable display of aerobatics the Frigate then spirals and catches the disgorged fish before it hits the ocean. Both birds breed on the atoll of Huvadu but not in any great numbers. The small colonies are subject to much disturbance from the islanders who collect the eggs and sometimes take the young birds. It is a long established custom for the islanders to capture the sea birds either for their flesh or more often to make pets of them and it is a common sight in all the villages to see birds around the gardens and houses. The eggs of the nesting sea birds are also taken and this is starting to become quite a pressure on the smaller populations of sea birds. The common noddy, *Anous stolidus pileatus*, and the lesser noddy, *Anous tenuirostris*, (Naaranga), are seen all up and down the islands usually out to sea. The fishermen keep an eager eye out for these birds as they can be relied upon to point out where the

tuna are concentrating. These birds are thought to breed in the southern atolls along with other sea birds like the boobys and gannets. Perhaps the most stunning of all Maldivian birds, the white tailed tropic bird, *Phaethon lepturus lepturus*, (Dhandifuli-Dooni) suffers more than any other because both the adults and eggs are taken during the breeding season. These superbly adapted oceanic birds with their long streaming tail feathers come to the islands to nest, usually choosing to do so under the thick and tangled roots of the screwpine trees where they fall easy prey to the islanders. Being fiercely protective and aggressive the bird on the nest will not desert but neither is it a match for a man. It is very likely that other tropic bird species are breeding in the Maldives but for them to continue to visit the islands they will have to be afforded some protection. It is possible that both the red-billed and the red-tailed tropic birds are visitors to the islands as well. Audubon's shearwater, *Procellaria iherminieri bailloni*, (Hoagulhaa) a small sturdily built sea bird, visits many of the islands to breed particularly along the eastern sea board and its eggs and the live birds are taken by the islanders.

Endemic mammalian fauna is restricted to a total of two species, both of which are members of the bat family. *Pteropus giganteus ariel* or as it is commonly known, the flying fox is to be found on the larger islands when it is not disturbed by human activity. These attractive creatures pick out the

Left, top: Large red hermit crab.

Bottom: Ghost crab. Common on the beaches of every island.

Above: Massive aggressive land crab. Rarely met with away from mangrove swamps in the far north.

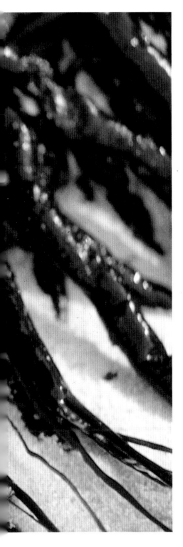

Left, top: A brightly coloured crab common on the foreshore.

Bottom: Tiny hermit crab.

Above: The small porcelain crab.

largest tree on the island where they form large roosts. In the early evenings they can be seen flying off to ravage the various fruit-trees of the villagers. They cause considerable damage to the fruit-crops but the islanders seem remarkably tolerant of their behaviour and make no effort to disturb or destroy the colonies. It is thought that this could be a distinctive form unique to the Maldives.

The other bat *Pteropus hypomelanus maris* is very rare and has only once been recorded from the southern atoll of Addu. Since the single specimen was discovered it has been searched for in vain, so this must remain as a tentative species for the Maldives.

The only other three mammals are all introductions that have arrived on ships over the years and are widespread throughout this area of the world. The house mouse and black rat are everywhere, with the rat in particular being a pest on all inhabited islands where it causes much damage to crops. The last is the Indian house shrew which is beneficial rather than harmful as it feeds on insects, spiders and other small creatures. Its high pitched call can be heard in most houses in Malé.

Marine Life

INTRODUCTION

Although the land flora and fauna of the Maldives is somewhat scarce the same certainly cannot be said about the undersea world of the islands. Without a doubt the Maldives have some of the most superb reef systems in the world, perhaps today ranking even higher than the Great Barrier Reef of Australia which has suffered so much recently from the ever advancing depredations of the crown of thorns starfish. The Maldivian reefs are much as they were many hundreds of years ago without a trace of industrial pollution.

Recently a few reefs have suffered around the Malé atoll because of the construction of tourist islands and the careless misuse of few divers and tourists who remove living elements of the reefs. Luckily the Maldivian government has been quick to recognise this and taken steps to ensure that the survival of the reefs is not compromised by the rapidly growing tourist industry. Tourists can help the situation and ensure the untroubled continuation of this marvellous natural monument by treating the coral reefs with the care and respect they deserve.

To dive under the sea of the Maldives is to be transported to another world where nature still holds sway over the balance of life, sometimes devastatingly beautiful and sometimes deadly.

The reefs are located a short swimming distance across the sandy shallow lagoons, where hardly cleared by the ocean one minute, the next they drop away in a steep cliff hundreds and sometimes thousands of feet deep. It is an uncanny experience to hang suspended in the warm water with, on one side, the safety and bulk of the reef over which lies the lagoon, whilst not a few feet away the waters plunge down to unknown depths where visibility is reduced to almost nothing.

Our knowledge of these reefs has grown considerably in the past 25 years but the vastness, complexity and sheer diversity of life here will always defeat the human mind. And this is part of the beauty and allure of the Maldivian reefs; there will always be something new to discover, something unknown to find.

With as many 200 different species of hard coral so far identified from the reefs around the islands, the Maldives has one of the richest areas to be found in the world, only beaten by the Philippines, Great Barrier Reef and a few other small islands such as the Chagos archipelago to the south.

Coral is a very general term used to describe a great variety of tiny animals belonging to the phylum, *Coelenterata*, and this basically means that all these related forms possess skeletal material situated in their living tissues or entirely enclosing the animal.

Most corals, when seen at close range, look like typical anemones, this living part is known as a polyp and is normally cylindrical in appearance with a size ranging from under a millimetre to several centimetres. The coral feeds by waving small tentacles, gathered around the mouth, which sweep microscopic animals into its digestive organs.

Reefs are built up by the living corals because as they grow they deposit excess skeletal material and over many thousands of years this achieves the type of reef in evidence around the islands of the Maldives. These are colonial corals and many different species, influenced by the light intensity and the force of the undersea swell, contribute to the formation of the reef. Quite different coral structures will be found in areas with a rough sea and areas with a calm sea; for instance in sandy lagoons the corals will be of a delicate form while coral structures on the sea side of the reef will be of a massive type. Light plays a major role in the development of these reefs and the form of the coral changes at different depths.

It can be confusing to identify individual species of coral as they have many different shapes and sizes and even more confusing they will appear with completely different colours. This is because much of the coral's colouring comes not from the living tissues of the coral itself but from invading algae that live in the polyps of the coral; they are able to impart red, green, yellow and brown colours to the coral. Various colours are produced by the corals themselves. The reefs are not made up solely from the corals, as many other forms of life also contribute to these

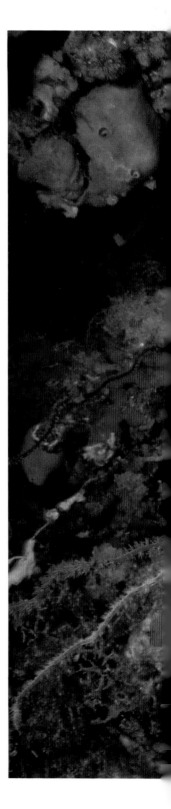

The dazzling and delicate beauty of the reefs. Pix: Dr.Chas Anderson

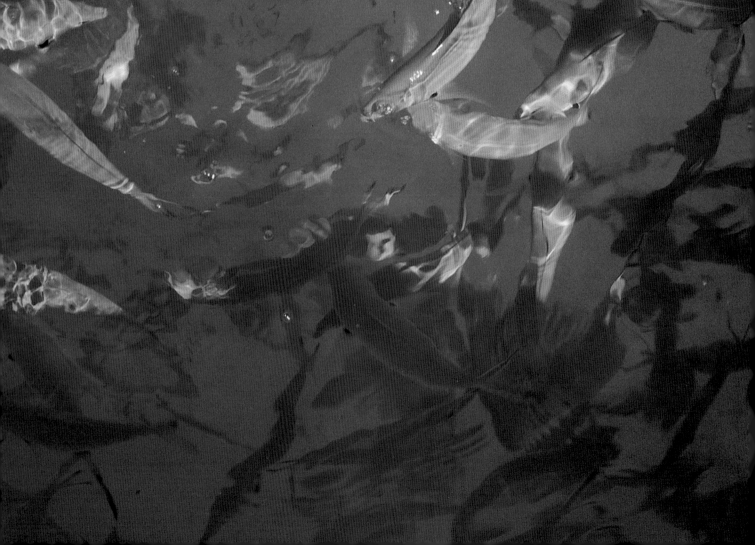

intricate constructions. Two forms of algae play a major part in holding the reef together, the green by leaving rough material and the red serving much the same purpose as the corals by growing as a hard calcified layer.

Soft corals are quite different from the hard forms in that they contain their skeletal material within the living tissues imparting a soft appearance which is very often of a stunning beauty.

The Maldivian reefs are bursting with a variety of lesser creatures whose sheer numbers defy description, for instance there are as many as 5,000 different species of shells occurring there. It is not within the scope of this book to attempt to enumerate every species that might be found, so mention will be made only of the commoner shells likely to be met with by swimmers or divers around the beaches and reefs.

Cowries are shells of the superfamily *Cypraeacea* distinguished by their gorgeous colours and neat shells. The incredible lustre of the shell is produced by the gastropod's mantle, which covers almost the entire shell area when expanded and coats it with minute chalk algae, which in their turn keep off other algae that would otherwise damage the shell. The design and colour of the shell is also produced by the constant actions of this mantle. Like most shells, cowries are active by night and tend to lay up during the day. They are most often found in shallower water.

Cone shells of the family *Conidae* are very common in Maldivian waters and out of the 1,500 species many can be found around the reefs. But a word of warning here, many cone shells are highly poisonous and should not be handled under any circumstances.

One of the largest shells of the region is the triton, a massive construction of over 400 mm from the family, *Cymatiidae*, which is a predatory shell living of starfish and crustacea. Its appearance, much like a giant ice cream cone, is obvious and it has a deep rich chocolate colour striped with ivory. This large shell is still used on some of the remoter islands to call the villagers to a meeting place. It is thought that there are as many as 2,000 different species of fish around the reefs of the Maldives and to catalogue and describe even a tenth of this number would require a separate book all to itself but the following pictures and their captions can serve as a good introduction to this marvellous underwater world.

Marine Life

The following section on the marine life of the Maldives has been written and illustrated by Dr Chas Anderson, a marine biologist who has spent many years studying and photographing the reefs of the Maldives.

1. The reefs of the Maldives, indeed the entire country, has been built over millions of years by countless tiny coral animals. Living corals secrete a limestone skeleton which remains behind when the animals die. It is these limestone skeletons that form the basis of all coral reefs. The coral animals contain within their tissues symbiotic algae (symbiosis is a term that literally means 'living together'). These algae, like other plants, use the energy of sunlight to carry out photosynthesis. The coral animals benefit from the extra food and oxygen produced in this way, and this is a major explanation for their prodigious reef building capacities. Reliance on symbiotic algae limits the reef building corals to the upper, sunlit layers of the tropical oceans. But within this zone the diversity of coral forms is bewildering, and they provide an ideal habitat for a staggering array of other creatures.

2

4

3

2. The living coral animal is called a polyp. Polyps are not normally visible because they are usually retracted during the day, only expanding to feed at night, and also because many are extremely small. These bright orange polyps of the coral Tubastrea are unusually large, being some three to four centimetres across, and have been photographed at night while fully expanded. On their outspread tentacles the polyps have numerous stinging cells with which they can immobilize small animals passing on the current. The hapless prey is then passed by the tentacles into the central mouth. Tubastrea feeds entirely in this manner, since it does not contain the symbiotic algae of the true reef building corals. It is also different from most of those forms in that the polyps are solitary, and not grouped together in colonies.

3. Most coral reefs support a wide variety of coral species, but there are some areas where just one or two species dominate. These foliaceous (leaf-like) corals are growing in the sheltered waters inside the atoll basin where there is no heavy wave action, and it is possible for such delicate growth forms to thrive. Notice how the coral plates grow out roughly horizontally so as to benefit from the maximum sunlight.

4. While the true, or stony, corals are the main builders of Maldivian reefs there are many other types of animal that are also important in the ecology of the living reefs. Among these are several groups of animals closely related to the true corals. These include the sea fans, or gorgonians, one of which is illustrated here. Sea fans are colonial animals with a fan shaped skeleton made

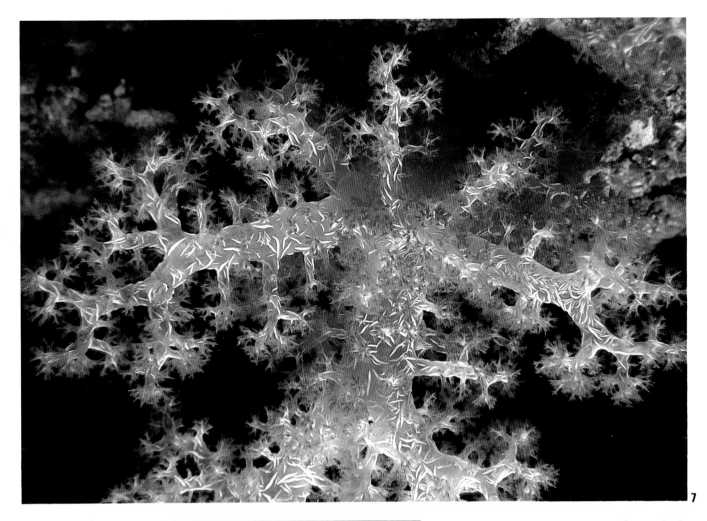

7

6

of a tough horn-like substance, from which numerous polyps protrude. In this case the skeleton is red, and the polyps are white. Sea fans are essentially two dimensional and typically grow across the current, i.e. perpendicular to the reef, so that the polyps are exposed to the greatest volume of passing water. They can grow to a considerable size, some species reaching well over two metres across.

5. The wire or whip-coral, *Cirripathes*, is another colonial coral-like animal with a horny central skeleton. Whip-corals are, however, more closely related to the semi-precious black corals than to the sea fans. This specimen is only about 30 cm long, but whip-corals can grow to several metres in length. Such specimens are usually loosely coiled, like over-sized springs.

6 & 7. Soft corals, as their name suggests, do not have a hard skeleton, either of limestone or horn. Instead, the colonial structure is fleshy or water-filled, with relatively minor strengthening being provided by numerous 'spicules' embedded in the colonial wall. Illustrated here are two colourful examples of soft corals, *Dendronephthya*. The red and orange colouration is provided by the feeding polyps; the spicules are bright white.

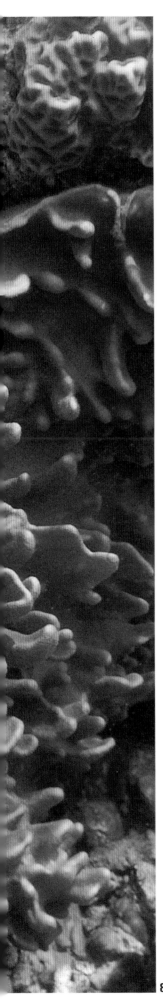

8. Competition for space on the crowded reef is acute. A mobile animal, hard pressed by competitors can always move to a new site, but sedentary species such as the corals and their relations cannot. They have therefore evolved many mechanisms to prevent other animals from growing over them. This illustration shows a hard coral (left) in danger of being overgrown by a faster growing softer coral (right). Soft corals excrete toxic chemicals, trying to kill off their neighbours. Hard corals can fight back with powerful stinging tentacles. The outcome of this particular 'battle' may not be decided for several months. At the time it was photographed, close observation of this encounter showed that the hard coral was successfully keeping the soft coral at bay, with no direct contact between the protagonists along the whole length of the 'battlefield'.

9. Apart from the various types of coral, there is a great diversity of other creatures living on the reefs. Among the simplest of the conspicuous reef animals are the sponges, such as this bright orange individual. Sponges are filter-feeders, drawing water into an internal cavity through hundreds of microscopic pores and then passing it out through the larger, visible holes. Despite the apparent paucity of edible matter in the water (hence its relative clarity) filter — feeding is a very common mode of life on the reef, and an ecologically very important one in that it helps to ensure efficient recycling of nutrients within the reef ecosystem.

11

10

12

10. Despite their rather humble appearance, ascidians or sea-squirts are zoologically-speaking quite advanced animals. They are structurally more complex than sponges, and they also have a far more complicated development. However, like sponges they live by filter-feeding. Many ascidians are solitary, but the ones shown here are colonial forms. The large hole at the top of each is a common pore through which filtered water is passed back into the sea. Water is drawn in through numerous small individual pores in the sides of the colonies.

11 & 12. Another important group of filter-feeding animals are the bivalve molluscs, which includes the familiar clams. They draw water in through one 'siphon', pass it across their gills, which therefore serve the dual functions of food as well as oxygen gathering, and then out through another siphon. Clams of the genus *Tridacna*, of which the famous giant clam is a member, greatly suppliment this source of nutrition by having symbiotic algae present in their tissues. By staying slightly ajar and exposing their fleshy 'mantles' to the sunlight the algae inside are able to carry out photosynthesis. As a result the clam receives extra food, just as the stony coral polyps do from their symbiotic algae.

13

14

15

13. A final example of the wide diversity of filter-feeding animals found on Maldivian coral reefs is provided by this gorgeously coloured featherstar. Featherstars are related to starfishes. They are mainly nocturnal, hiding in crevices by day but crawling out at dusk to feed on the abundant nighttime plankton. Featherstars actually have two sets of arms: the highly visible large 'feathery' ones that are used for both feeding and locomotion, and a smaller set underneath that are used for grasping the substrate. This they sometimes have to do most tenaciously since featherstars often climb up onto the top of rocks or other animals such as seafans in areas of the reef most exposed to currents in order to improve their chances of catching food.

14. Most starfishes, such as this colourful *Fromia*, are omnivorous scavengers, feeding on a variety of material on the reef surface. An exception is the notorious crown-of-thorns starfish which feeds on living corals. Many starfish are essentially nocturnal, presumably because they are subject to predation by day-active fish.

15. Small hermit crabs are a common sight on most Maldivian beaches, but large ones are normally only seen underwater. There are many species of hermit crab. Most are scavengers, feeding on such things as dead fish. Their soft abdomens are tucked into abandoned gastropod (snail) shells, which they carry around with them, withdrawing into them for protection whenever necessary. This hermit crab, *Dardanus*, has *Calliactis* sea anemones on its shell.

17

18

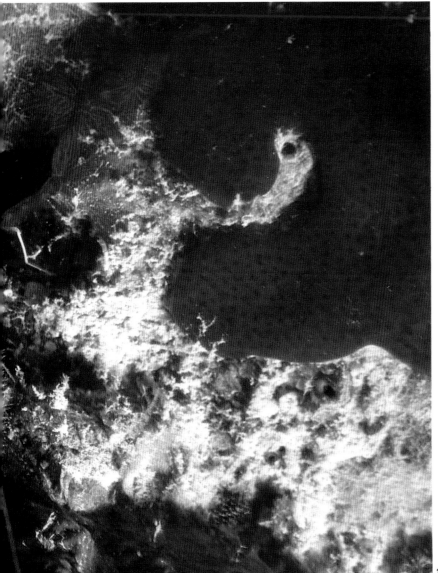

16

16. The banded coral shrimp, *Stenopus*, is a common and distinctive member of the reef fauna. They often occur in pairs and usually stand just inside small crevices, from which their long white antennae protrude. Fish are attracted to these antennae, and allow themselves to be cleaned by the shrimps, which climb all over them picking off parasites.

17. While the variety of 'lower' life forms on coral reefs is unsurpassed in the oceans, it is the diversity of fish life that really catches the attention. Among the fish of the tropical coral reefs perhaps the most famous, or infamous, are the sharks. Most people's fear of sharks is, however, ill-founded. Indeed the average visitor to the Maldives should count himself lucky to even see a shark. Divers who visit the few sites that sharks regularly frequent may see several at one time, but otherwise sharks are rarely seen underwater. If they are seen it is normally just a glimpse as one swims past in the distance, like this requiem shark, *Carcharinus*.

18. Moray eels, of which there are many species, are also important predators on the reef. They feed mainly at night, hunting through the cracks and crevices for fish, which they can detect with their acute sense of smell. As befits animals that live in this way, morays have strong bodies and very sharp teeth. They do not bother swimmers or divers unless provoked. However, Maldivian fishermen fear morays more than any other fish, because once hooked they fight ferociously, especially when brought into the boat. They can stay alive and snapping long after they have been landed, which can make removing the hook a very risky business.

19. The rock cods or groupers, of which this vermilion rock cod, *Cephalopholis miniata*, is a representative, are another important group of predatory fishes, although far less fearsome than either the sharks or the morays. The rock cods are mainly 'lie-in-wait' predators. They remain motionless for long periods of time until a shrimp or small fish passes in front of them, when they gulp it down with lightning speed.

20 & 21. The lionfish, *Pterois*, and the scorpionfish, *Scorpaenopsis*, are closely related. Both feed on small fish and crustaceans that unwarily come too close to their waiting jaws. Both also have a row of poisonous spines along their backs. For a large predatory fish is just as happy eating a small predatory fish as a small herbivorous fish, and with so many carnivores about a wide variety of protective mechanisms have been evolved. But while the scorpionfish is remarkably well camouflaged, presumably to improve its chances of catching prey, the lionfish is flamboyantly decorative, possibly to advertise its venomous spines and discourage potential predators.

19

22

22. Another common protective strategy is that of forming schools. The advantages of doing so include the fact that it allows many eyes to keep a look out for would-be predators, and that it is very difficult for a predator to pick out and attack one victim in the confusion of a swirling school. The blue-lined snapper, *Lutjanus kasmira*, forms large stationary schools during the day. At night these schools break up and the individual fish hunt along the reef for their crustacean prey.

23. The anemone fishes, *Amphiprion*, have adapted yet another protective strategy. These little fishes live in close association with giant sea anemones. When threatened by a predator the anemone fish seeks shelter among the tentacles of the anemone, which are armed with stinging cells. The anemone fish itself is coated with a layer of mucus which gives it immunity from the action of the stinging cells. What benefit, if any, the anemone gets from the association is not clear, but there are reports of anemone fish dropping food on to the anemone, and driving away butterflyfish which might eat parts of the anemone.

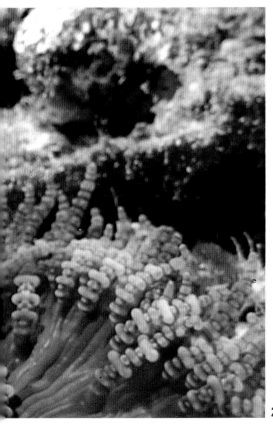

23

25

24 & 25. Among the most beautiful of all the reef inhabitants are the angelfishes. These two species are the Empress angelfish, *Pygoplites diacanthus*, and the Imperial angelfish, *Pomocanthus imperator*. Both species feed mainly on sponges and other encrusting organisms. They are normally seen singly, for they are somewhat territorial and will exclude other individuals from their home ranges. By contrast, the related butterflyfishes are normally seen in pairs or small groups.

26. Butteflyfishes can most readily be distinguished from angelfishes by their lack of a strong cheek spine, but they also differ in more fundamental matters, including larval development. This species is the teardrop butterflyfish, *Chaetodon unimaculatus*. It feeds mainly on corals. Different butterflyfish species feed on different things, and their mouths are adapted to their particular feeding modes. Some species, for example, have greatly protruding mouths which enable them to pick small animals out of tiny crevices in the coral.

26

24

27

27. Parrotfishes are so called because of their strong beaks and bright colours. They feed by rasping algal growths off coral rocks. In doing so, quantities of coral rock are inevitably ingested as well. This is ground down by powerful sets of teeth in the throat in order to facilitate digestion of the organic material. The waste product is sand, which is produced in enormous quantities. Parrotfishes are ecologically important because, by keeping the growth of the algae down they allow young corals to grow.

The Maldivian islands provide an ideal refuge for the turtle and various species are relatively common around the reefs; the commonest is the hawksbill turtle, *Eretmochelys imbricata* (Velaa), but even these have witnessed a drop in their population over the last ten years. The females come ashore to lay their eggs on the soft sandy beaches in carefully excavated pits, where they will lay as many as 150 eggs. The females will visit the beaches three or four times and lay as many as a 1000 eggs in these different nests between the months of June to November; the young hatch out after dark and are particularly vulnerable as they make their way to the sea with predatory fish and birds picking them off easily. Turtles can swim at astonishing speeds, 50kph not being unusual and in the case of the giant leatherback turtle as fast as 74kph. Turtles are omnivorous creatures feeding on almost anything they find including coral and are often seen scavenging along the reefs.

The bottlenose dolphin *Tursiops truncatus*, is abundant in the Maldives and almost at anytime, anywhere it is possible to see large schools of these mammals sporting and swimming at the edge of the reef. They are torpedo-shaped animals of a dark grey colour with a long and broad dorsal fin and the distinctive broad and long beak which gives the animal its name. Feeding on a variety of fish and crustaceans they represent no danger to man and are one of the most delightful animals to encounter.

Above: Probably the most beautiful reefs in the world.

Plant Life

This section is written and illustrated by Dr Dennis Adams of the British Museum of Natural History who has made an extensive survey of the flora and is probably the only authority on the subject.

The atolls have been formed solely from the growth of coral and it is the broken and crushed calcareous skeletons of these marine animals, thrown up on their own reefs, that have provided the building material of the islands. At first there is only coral rubble in which smaller particles derived from crumbled shells and algae lodge. A sandbank may develop under the influence of winds and waves and some part of it eventually remains above sea-level at all times. In these situations plants colonise in an extremely limited range of environmental opportunities. The pioneers are necessarily salt tolerant beach-loving or mangrove species.

As the island increases in size different types of vegetation become possible. There is diversified relief, gradual reduction of salinity associated with rainwater collection and storage and, later, evolution of soil. Islands often become saucer-shaped with sometimes a swamp or even a pond in the central depression. This results, generally, in there being richer soils towards the middle of the island. These soils gradually acquire more organic content after plants have been established on them for some time; they are darker, have greater water retention and lower pH (7.0-7.8) than the peripheral soils which are less fertile due to excess of calcareous sand imparting extreme alkalinity (pH up to 8.8) and more rapid drainage.

Older islands develop underlying impervious layers of fine sand and clay hardened chemically through the interaction of dissolved salts and eluted humic matter. These layers assist the storage of fresh water in subterranean sumps by keeping rainwater and seawater apart. As islands change shape and position these layers may become exposed as beach rock, which has some characters of mineral rock but is nevertheless organic in origin. There is no modern mention of the great quantities of pumice which fell

Left: Guettarda speciosa (uni).

Above: Cordia subcordata (kaani).

on the Maldives after the eruption of Krakatau (now named Rakata) in the Sunda Strait in 1883. J. Stanley Gardiner described in 1901 how islanders would gather baskets of pumice to place around the roots of plaintains and other food plants to improve nutrition.

The mature soils are usually rich in phosphorus and magnesium but low in nitrogen, potash and trace elements. Deficiency of manganese and excess of calcium, preventing uptake of minerals from the soil, cause chlorosis (loss of green colour) in certain

ditions. Sufficient supply of freshwater, both for plants and human habitation, requires adequate areas of catchment and this depends on maintaining maximum soil surface open to the sky. Against the foregoing physical background the islands show patterns of vegetation cover depending on their size, age and degree of human disturbance. The very uniform appearance of most islands when viewed from some distance away is imparted by the almost ubiquitous coconut palms. These useful trees are the first objects to come into sight over the horizon

plants. Such evidence of deficiency can be seen in wild species as well as cultivated plants growing in less fertile places.

Most plants are intolerant of saline conditions which means their roots must have access to fresh water. In Maldive conditions deep-rooted trees would ultimately reach seawater beneath the island and would not thrive. Gardiner stated, 'There are no mango trees; a few young plants in Malé. The introduction of this tree had been tried many times but it will not flourish'. Mango seedlings and saplings have long vertical taproots; the fact that there are today many massive mature mango trees in Malé is explained by extra care being taken during early growth, especially watering, until widespreading lateral roots have grown out. These horizontal roots can exploit superficial layers of soil and pick up rain as soon as it falls. This is a fact of life for many tropical trees and other plants. Coconut trees and Pandanus have numerous adventitious roots which are continually being replaced and this contributes to their success in Maldive con

as one approaches an island by boat and the distance of the first sighting is determined by their height. A coconut palm can grow to 30 metres but it is doubtful if many examples in these islands exceed 20 metres. However, it is rare for any other tree to reach this height let alone overtop. If this does occur it is most often by a banyan fig (*Ficus benghalensis*). When such a fig tree is present not only can the island be spotted from a greater distance but it also becomes an aid to navigation and identification. Very young islands, without palms or other significant trees, come into view only at much shorter range.

There are five categories of vegetation present in these islands into which the native plants have grouped themselves ecologically. One might say that preference for a particular kind of site determines to which category any species belongs but some plants are more tolerant of a wider range of conditions than others and very few species are strictly confined to one situation only:

1. Beach Pioneers
The first plants encountered on coming

Left: Beach with pioneer vegetation.

Above, left: Acrostichum aureum.

Right: Tacca leontopetaloides (hiththala).

ashore at a natural beach are mostly the same as those which colonise newly formed sandbanks. They are known as beach pioneers. There are about twenty characteristic species and because sandy beaches are universal, several of them have pantropical distribution. The plants tend to be low and herbaceous; about half of them are grasses or sedges, collectively referred to as 'hui' in these islands. They may have tufted or creeping growth. The non-grasses often have succulent leaves and the commonest of them is *Launaea sarmentosa* (kulhafilaa) with

clusive patches but more often the hedge is narrow and the species are intermingled.

3. Sublittoral Thicket

Behind the beaches in well drained areas not completely dominated by coconuts, the natural tendency is for a community of small trees to develop. This zone is often quite distinct, requiring longer to establish and comprising more salt-sensitive species. About twenty common species of mixed life form include shrubs, climbers and shade-tolerant grasses. The prevalent trees are *Cordia subcordata* (kaani), *Guettarda*

rosettes of edible leaves at intervals along trailing stolons. All the species are highly salt-tolerant.

Where the beach is being deposited and the plants are still affected directly by wave action, stabilizing grasses such as *Lepturus* or *Thuarea* may be present; where a beach is being washed away *Pemphis acidula* (kuredi) is the commonest small woody plant to be found with its roots actually in the sea. Where a beach is fully stabilized the beach pioneers may be accompanied along the inner part of the zone by seedlings or small saplings of the plants of the littoral hedge.

2. Littoral Hedge

Although not always clearly recognizable as a zone, some of the species are universally present along the upper beach. The usual growth form is shrubby with numerous branches and these may be lax or trailing. There are ten or so common species of which the most constant are *Scaevola sericea*, the small kind of Pandanus and *Pemphis acidula*. When the formation is extensive, these plants have often spread into mutually ex-

speciosa (uni), *Hibiscus tiliaceus* (diggaa) and *Premna obtusifolia* (kude). These trees rarely exceed five metres in most of the situations where they occur and they are accompanied frequently by climbers, especially *Canavalia cathartica* (maanifa).

4. Climax Forest

Where more moist undisturbed conditions pertain, an optimum forest (climax) may be found. This comprises mature trees from the foregoing community as well as *Hernandia nymphaeifolia* (kandhu), and *Terminalia catappa* (midhili) and, on some islands, the large Pandanus. This is the most luxuriant and complex vegetation occurring in these islands as it includes additional life forms such as *Cirnum* (bondi kadhollu) and ground orchids of the genus *Eulophia*. The existence of epiphytic orchids, as mentioned by T. Heyerdahl, 'The Maldive Mystery', 1986, has not been confirmed in any botanical investigations made so far.

The islands are mostly too small or too disturbed by the planting of coconuts or other human activity for the inland com-

Left, top: Crinum asiaticum (kandholho).

Bottom: Ripe fruit of the small Pandanus.

Above: Thuarea involuta.

munities always to be clearly distinguishable; they tend to run into one another anyway and some common species of native tree such as Calophyllum inophyllum (funa), can occupy all habitats from the mature forest to the beach. In other situations introduced trees such as breadfruit or bambukeyo, *Artocarpus altilis*, grow to great size and support epiphytes or shelter the rarer ground herbs of the climax.

5. Mangrove and Swamp Forest

The forest community occupying depressions is rather more distinct. It is determined by constant surface water and, according to salinity, may be typical mangrove with trees having modified roots, or swamp forest comprising unmodified trees tolerant of brackish conditions.

The former may have pure stands of *Rhizophora mucronata* with long arching prop roots which can establish mangrove forest on rough coral rubble while still immersed in the seawater. Other mangroves like *Bruguiera* or *Sonneratia* have finger-like upright branches on their roots. The swamp forests may have massive *Barringtonia asiatica* (kimbi) trees and the very common and widespread *Morinda citrifolia* (ahi). In more open places mangrove fern, *Acrostichum aureum* and long-leaved herbs such as Cladium (baiypouburu) and Typha (lonsi) are gregarious. Variation in the density of floristic composition of any kind of vegetation may be expected depending on the nature of the substrate, whether sand, coral rubble or humus-rich soil, and also on moisture. Southern islands generally have higher rainfall and a more luxuriant plant life.

Left, top: Scaevola sericea (maagoo). The most common plant used for firewood.

Bottom: Forked stems of the large Pandanus (kashi keyo) used as props for boats.

This page: Hernandia nymphaeifolia. (kandhu)

THE ORIGINS OF THE NATIVE FLORA

The number of species which have reached these islands on their own is relatively small. By combining published lists with findings from recent studies, the total tally of species is nearly 600, of which over half are known only in cultivation, either as food or other economic plants or as shade trees or ornamentals.

The number of truly native or fully naturalized species is fewer than 260. Of these, many are pantropical weeds which accompany human activity and were not necessarily introduced for any good reason. This leaves a very small truly indigenous component — probably fewer than 100 species that would have inhabited the islands before human settlement.

It may be significant that, even with all the introductions taken into account, there are more islands in the Maldives than there are kinds of plants reported in them. This is in stark contrast to the situation in, for example, the Caribbean or Fiji where several hundred islands are occupied by thousands of species of plants. The difference is, of course, due to the more varied physiography in those other islands creating many more niches for plants to occupy.

In earlier times there was much wonderment and speculation about how such distant islands acquired their wild floras and faunas. These days much is known about the distribution of plants and the remarkable thing about the Maldives is that almost all the common native species also occur in the coral islands of the Pacific Ocean in identical habitats, while many of them are rare or absent in the intervening areas. In a recent book on coastal plants of the tropical Pacific (Whistler 1980) forty-nine of the sixty-eight species (72%) are in common with these islands, extending over remarkable distances of ocean of from five to ten thousand miles. If we study the ocean currents between the Pacific and Indian Oceans, it is clear that the most economical routes in time and distance would put the Maldives at the receiving end of species originating in the Pacific rather than vice versa.

The ecology of the special adaptations of these plants to the extreme limitations of life on small coral islands is matched by their modifications for long-distance dispersal. The simple fact is that their seeds or fruits float and are able to survive in seawater. The bouyancy is achieved in different ways but a common method is for the fruit to have a fibrous layer in its wall like a coconut. This adaptation has evolved independently in otherwise unrelated groups of plants. Yet other plants have been shown to be transported for great distances by birds and a few by the wind, but the most efficient means is by floatation and this is in keeping with the remoteness of coral atolls separated by vast expanses of ocean.

The lack of ecological opportunity, together with the high dispersal potential of the true natives, accounts for the negligible occurrence of species restricted solely to these islands. Gardiner wrote, 'The flora of the Maldives.....proves to contain no peculiar forms.' Subsequently to this statement the local representatives of the important genus, Pandanus, the screwpines of the Pacific area, have been assigned to five species all of which are said not to occur anywhere else. In other words, the only endemic plants in the whole flora are those species of Pandanus. That contention creates a problem which must be resolved before any definitive account of the Maldives flowering plants can be compiled. There is an inconsistency emphasized by the fact that the fruits of Pandanus are among the most efficient for dispersal over long sea distances and as flotsam are therefore highly likely to have reached other shores. The local people recognise only three kinds which are referred to simply as small, medium and large. Moreover, the awareness of these plants is anything but casual because they are put to many uses. Further study and more careful comparison with plants in other countries is needed.

Left: Launaea sarmentosa. (kulhafilaa)

Bottom: Calophyllum inophyllum (funa).

115

ECONOMIC AND CULTIVATED PLANTS

Apart from coconuts which are everywhere used for food, oil, fibre, lumber and shelter, crops have varied over the years in response to changing needs and economic circumstances. Fishing normally takes precedence over all other activities, but in a few places where agriculture is more profitable fishing may become secondary. In some islands there is seasonal alternation between these activites. In other communities fishing is carried out from the home island and agriculture, as well as the collection of firewood, mainly obtained from *Scaevola sericea* (magu), is undertaken on nearby uninhabited islands.

Only about five percent of the land surface of the islands is suitable for arable farming. There are a few goats in some places but there are no grazing or browsing animals. Principal field crops are finger millet, *Eleusine corocana* (binbi) and Italian millet, *Setaria italica* (kudibai). Rice is not grown at this time but is imported in large quantities, paid for by fish export. Sorghum, *Sorghum bicolor* (donalha) is another grain that is sometimes grown.

Tuber crops include sweet potato — *Ipomoea batatas* (kattala) and, especially in the south, taro — *Colocasia esculenta* (goboliala). Chillis — *Capsicum annuum* (mirus), small onion — Allium cepa (kudifia), manioc or cassava — *Manihot esculenta* (dandialuvi), watermelon — *Citrullus lanatus* (karaa), pineapple — *Ananas comosus* (alanaasi), betel-leaf-*Piper betle* (bileiy) a vine, and other garden crops are grown

Left: **Small Pandanus** (medu keyo).

Right : **Scaevola sericea** (magoo).

117

locally and sporadically. Breadfruit — *Arto-carpus altilis* (bambukea) is grown on all inhabited islands; other fruit trees including banana — *Musa hybrid* (faiy keo), citrus-mostly lime — *Citrus aurantifolia* (lumboa) and areca nut-*Areca catechu* (foah) are grown in houseyards or on a larger scale on some of the more suitable islands. An interesting standby for a starchy vegetable is the Indian arrowroot — *Tacca leontopetaloides* (hith-thala) which is fully naturalized if not native in sandy thickets on almost all the islands and is sometimes grown domestically.

Medicinal herbs are obtained from wild sources and others, along with spices, are grown for local use. Yet others are imported and sold in the markets.

Non-food uses of plant products are numerous. The retting, shredding and twist-ing of coir is carried out on all the islands, the preparation of rope being mainly done by women. Some selected varieties of coconut have unusually long fibres suitable for this purpose. Importation of nylon cord is a threat to the occupation.

Pandanus leaves were hitherto woven into sails but this material has now largely been replaced; screens, walls, mats and roofing (cadjan) are still made from this or from the leaves of the coconut palm. The Maldive is-lands are famous for the mats (kunaa) woven with the stems of native sedges (haiburu — mostly *Pycreus polystachyos*) coloured with native dyes obtained from other plants. Cotton — *Gossypium spp* (kafa) is grown on a much smaller scale than in the past.

Perfumes are obtained from the roots of khus-khus — *Vetiveria zizanioides* (Lan-

Left: Areca catechu (fen). Areca nut.

This page, top: Pemphis acidula.

119

**Above: Cool and well
planted Malé house and
garden.**

simoo), from the introduced citronella grass
and lemon grass — *Cymbopogon spp* and
from the flowers fo the native wuni — *Guettarda speciosa*, and introduced frangipani —
Plumeria spp.

Hardwoods are very scarce and where
available they are used for lime burning;
seasoned coconut is used to build the hulls of
the 'dhonis', the individual planks being fixed
together with the durable resilient dowels of
Pemphis acidula (kuredi).

It is only in recent years that much interest has been taken in ornamental plants,
but nowadays there is, at least in Malé, quite
a strong and growing group of peolpe engaged in decorative horticulture both as to
attractive trees and shrubs as well as pot-
plants in and around the house.